HERETICS AND
RENEGADES

by the same author

STALIN:
A Political Biography

RUSSIA AFTER STALIN

SOVIET TRADE UNIONS

THE PROPHET ARMED
(*Trotsky 1879–1921*)

THE PROPHET OUTARMED

THE GREAT CONTEST

THE PROPHET OUTCAST

IRONIES OF HISTORY

ISAAC DEUTSCHER

HERETICS AND RENEGADES

And Other Essays

WITH A NEW INTRODUCTION BY

E. H. CARR

THE BOBBS-MERRILL COMPANY, INC.
Indianapolis and New York

FIRST PUBLISHED IN THE UNITED STATES BY
COWARD-MCCANN IN 1957 UNDER THE TITLE
Russia in Transition

RE-ISSUED, WITH A NEW INTRODUCTION, 1969
INTRODUCTION © 1969 BY E. H. CARR

LIBRARY OF CONGRESS CATALOG NUMBER
LC 75-80739

Printed in Great Britain
The Bobbs-Merrill Company, Inc.
A Subsidiary of Howard W. Sams & Co., Inc., Publishers
Indianapolis - Kansas City - New York

DK
274
D4
1969

CONTENTS

INTRODUCTION

ISAAC DEUTSCHER'S early and lamented death in August 1967 has prompted among the wide circle of his readers and admirers a desire to review his work as a whole. In any final assessment, the time for which has scarcely yet arrived, the numerous essays and articles contributed by him to a large variety of journals and newspapers throughout the world may, perhaps, weigh lightly in comparison with the great biographies of Stalin and Trotsky. But he devoted a great deal of time and thought to them; they were written simultaneously with the major works; and they form a substantial part of his literary legacy. Many of them had already been collected and reprinted during his lifetime. *Heretics and Renegades* is the re-issue of a volume originally published in 1955.

The achievements and failures of the Russian revolution of 1917 were Isaac Deutscher's all-absorbing theme; it was his outstanding and almost unique merit that he could bring a balanced and profound appreciation both to the one and to the other. It was this which made him a controversial figure, and determined his position—midway between the dogmatic and fanatical devotees and the dogmatic and implacable critics—among writers on communism and on Soviet affairs. He never revisited the Soviet Union after the early nineteen thirties; and his name and writings have never been mentioned in the Soviet press except, on rare occasions, in terms of opprobrium. But, since fanatical devotees of the Soviet Union have almost ceased to exist in the English-speaking world in the last two decades, it was with the implacable enemies of the regime that he found himself most often at odds in his writings. Among these critics, ex-communists were commonly the most embittered and the most persistent.

Some of these spearheaded most of the attacks on his work.

The title *Heretics and Renegades* recalls this conflict of ideas, though it applies only to the first section of the volume—or, more strictly, to its first item, a review of the once famous book *The God that Failed*, in which nearly twenty years ago six well-known former communists set forth their disillusionment with the cause they had once embraced. Of the six, Ignazio Silone is by far the most sympathetic and persuasive—in part, no doubt, as Deutscher points out, because his membership of the communist party dated back to its earliest and genuinely idealistic period; those who joined communist parties in the already more cynical atmosphere of the nineteen thirties became Stalinists when they became communists, and as ex-communists are, in Deutscher's telling phrase, 'Stalinists in reverse'.

But the essay in this section which most people will be most eager to re-read is devoted not to an ex-communist, but to another disillusioned adherent of the Left, George Orwell, in the form of a review of his last novel *1984*. The essay analyses Orwell's sources—primarily Zamyatin's novel *We* which he had read in a French translation—and offers an extraordinarily subtle and fair-minded study of Orwell's aims and of the ambiguities of his picture, based both on a long-standing antipathy to the western society which he knew so well and on a more recently acquired detestation of the Russian society which he knew by report. *1984* is seen as a distillation of Orwell's 'boundless despair', announcing the advent of 'the Black Millennium, a Millennium of damnation'.

It would not be right for me to pass over in silence the long review, written in 1954 and here reprinted, of the first five volumes of my *History of Soviet Russia*, especially as it throws many sidelights on Isaac Deutscher's own view of early Soviet history. He calls me 'a great respecter of policies and a despiser—sometimes—of revolutionary ideas and principles', and speaks of my 'impatience with

Utopias, dreams, and revolutionary agitation'. Any such
bias I should now strive to correct. But does not Deutscher
lean to the other side? Are not his eyes sometimes so
firmly fixed on revolutionary Utopias and revolutionary
ideas as to overlook the expediencies which often governed
policy—even in the Lenin period? This is conspicuously
true of his criticism of my story of the Soviet-German
negotiations leading up to Rapallo. To read back into
these events the Stalinist moods of 1939 would, of course,
be a total anachronism; Soviet Russia at this time did not
think of a recovery of the territories lost to Poland. But if
Deutscher could have read the numerous records in the
German archives of conversations with Chicherin, Kopp
and other Soviet negotiators, before and after Rapallo, he
would not have written that the German dream of
'Poland's dismemberment with Russian help . . . evoked
no response in Soviet diplomacy or in the Bolshevik
leadership', or that Soviet statesmen were unwilling to
'play the Polish card'. After the Polish invasion of 1920,
fear and mistrust of a Poland swollen by her Versailles and
post-Versailles acquisitions loomed larger than any revolutionary ideas that might have inhibited a deal with the
Weimar republic.

But Isaac Deutscher's dedication to the principles of
the revolution, though it may have led him into an occasional one-sided interpretation, was an immense source of
strength. In the running battle, which generally ends in
compromise, between principle and expediency, Utopianism and realism, faith and cynicism, optimism and despair,
he stood unwaveringly on the side of the first. As the heir
both of the Enlightenment and of Marxism, he believed
firmly in reason and in the possibility of extending rational
control over human destinies. This is today a rare and
unfashionable view. But scarce commodities are all the
more valuable. It was this belief which inspired his searching critique of George Orwell's despair, and made him in
the last fifteen years of his life so much more effective a
student of Soviet affairs than the multitude of critics who

have sought to discredit his Utopianism and his optimism.

Isaac Deutscher understood more clearly than most that the vast industrial expansion of Soviet Russia in the last forty years, the spread of social services and of education —literacy for all, and higher education for an ever-widening circle of administrators, managers and policy-makers—had transformed society from top to bottom, and created new forces and new demands which must one day break forth. With quick insight he perceived—and wrote in public within a few days of Stalin's death—that the end of Stalin must also spell the end of Stalinism by releasing these cramped and stifled forces of revolt and reform. These prognostications, which have in the main been fully justified by the event, were the theme of *Russia After Stalin*, published in 1953.

When *Heretics and Renegades* was published in 1955, the Khrushchev era had scarcely begun and the sensational revelations of the twentieth party congress were still a year ahead. It was a moment of transition. In the varied fare provided in this volume three articles stand out as illustrating the atmosphere of the time—a picture of the last years of Stalin's rule written in 1951, a reply to critics of *Russia After Stalin*, and a description of the first months of the literary thaw after 1953. A fourth article, written within a few days of Beria's downfall, is one of Deutscher's rare excursions into Kremlinology—the art of speculating on the personal role of individual leaders—a *genre* which he generally eschewed. His strong point was always the analysis of the long-term trend, not of the sensational episode of the moment.

Throughout these articles Isaac Deutscher's message remains one of hope. At the height of the Stalin cult 'it looked as if Russian history had come to a standstill.' Yet this was an optical illusion: 'the appearance of stagnation concealed an immense movement.' After Stalin's death and the thaw, he wrote, 'a *prolonged* relapse into Stalinism is highly improbable'; for history had here 'opened a new chapter on Russia'. The Stalinist strait-jacket 'fitted an essentially primitive, pre-industrial society engaged in feverish industrialization and collectivization'. But 'a modern industrial nation cannot allow its creative energies to be so constricted, unless it is prepared to pay the penalty of ultimate stagnation.' The ambiguities of the situation were summed up in a telling phrase: 'The present social structure of the Soviet Union is already established too firmly to be undone, but not firmly enough to function altogether of its own accord, without coercion from above.'

The issue was undecided when these articles were written; and, in spite of many dramatic changes of fortune in the intervening decade, it remains undecided today. Yet, in the comparatively brief historical period of fifteen years since Stalin's death, an immense transformation has come over the Russian scene. The cynics and pessimists who believed that the revolution had been frozen by Stalin into an unbreakable totalitarian mould have been refuted. Khrushchev was not simply a Stalin in fancy dress; and the caution and hesitation of the present leaders do not conceal the ferment beneath. It seems unlikely that so forceful and turbulent a people, so recently emerged from the experience of revolution, will settle down to an altogether uneventful and monotonous process of stagnation. It seems unlikely that the spirit of the revolution, and the Utopian visions which it fostered, have entirely disappeared from the consciousness of the new generation; and, if this is true, solid grounds remain for the faith and optimism of which Isaac Deutscher was so persuasive an expositor.

Trinity College   E. H. CARR
Cambridge

PREFACE

SOME of the essays included in this volume appear here for the first time; others were written for various British, American, and French periodicals. The greater part of this collection consists of frankly controversial writings; and the whole of it is concerned with the most controversial issue of our time: Soviet society. I would like to think that although written at various times and from different angles these essays do possess a certain unity of idea which binds their separate strands of thought into something like an unpremeditated pattern. But I am also aware that by presenting them in book form I am inevitably exposing to scrutiny the oscillations of my thought over the years. However, only dead minds do not oscillate; and the oscillations of my own views do not perhaps go beyond limits compatible with a basic consistency of approach.

I have tried to oppose an analytical, sociological and historical view of Soviet society to the ex-Communists' lamentations over the 'God' that failed them and to their cries of despair and denunciation. The reader may detect the same key note—a note of *nil desperandum*—running through this book, from the reflections on the 'Ex-Communist's Conscience', set down in the United States early in 1950 in the heated atmosphere of the Hiss trial, through the piece on Orwell, written during the controversy over *1984* which has stirred the British public recently, to the survey of the 'Post-Stalin Ferment of Ideas' with which this volume ends.

Awareness of historical perspective seems to me to provide the best antidote to excessive pessimism as well as extravagant optimism over the great problems of our time (at least as long as we do not think about the danger of mankind's self-destruction by nuclear weapons, a danger for which the historian can know no precedent). The 'Historical Essays' and many passages scattered over the rest of the book attempt in particular to correlate the experience of the Russian revolution with that of the great French revolution and to find out where history has repeated itself and where it has refused to do so. Another group of papers scrutinizes the economic and social background of the Soviet Union during the close of the Stalin era. The concluding section of the book 'Russia in Transition' contains a partly hypothetical explanation of the Beria affair which, written in July 1953, anticipated clearly enough the fall of Malenkov. This essay was written as a Postscript to my book *Russia After Stalin* for its various, European and Asian, editions; and British readers have so far known it mostly from excerpts published in *The Times*.

Of the articles and essays which I have written in the course of a wide, at times vehement, international controversy over *Russia After Stalin*, I am including here only a reply to my French critics. One point in it may now be of greater interest than it was at the time of writing, namely the discussion of the international implications of the rise of the military influence in the post-Stalin regime.

I am greatly indebted to Mr. Donald Tyerman for giving me the benefit of his discriminating judgment and patient advice in the selection of these essays.

My thanks are due to the Editors of *The Times*, *The Times Literary Supplement*, *The Listener*, *Soviet Studies*, *The Reporter* (New York), *Foreign Affairs* (New York), and *Esprit* (Paris) for permission to reprint articles which appeared in their pages.

I.D.

15 *February* 1955
Coulsdon, Surrey.

PART ONE

HERETICS AND RENEGADES

THE EX-COMMUNIST'S CONSCIENCE[1]

IGNAZIO SILONE relates that he once said jokingly to Togliatti, the Italian Communist leader: 'The final struggle will be between the communists and the ex-communists.' There is a bitter drop of truth in the joke. In the propaganda skirmishes against the U.S.S.R. and communism, the ex-communist or the ex-fellow traveller is the most active sharpshooter. With the peevishness that distinguishes him from Silone, Arthur Koestler makes a similar point: 'It's the same with all you comfortable, insular, Anglo-Saxon anti-communists. You hate our Cassandra cries and resent us as allies—but, when all is said, we ex-communists are the only people on your side who know what it's all about.'

The ex-communist is the problem child of contemporary politics. He crops up in the oddest places and corners. He buttonholes you in Berlin to tell the story of *his* 'battle of Stalingrad', fought here, in Berlin, against Stalin. You find him in de Gaulle's entourage: none other than André Malraux, the author of *Man's Estate*. In America's strangest political trial the ex-communist has, for months, pointed his finger at Alger Hiss. Another ex-communist, Ruth Fischer, denounces her brother, Gerhart Eisler, and castigates the British for not having handed him back to the United States. An ex-Trotskyite, James Burnham, flays the American business man for his real or illusory lack of capitalist class consciousness, and sketches a programme of action for nothing less than the world-wide defeat of communism. And now six

[1] This essay appeared as a review of *The God That Failed* in *The Reporter* (New York) in April 1950.

writers—Koestler, Silone, André Gide, Louis Fischer, Richard Wright, and Stephen Spender—get together to expose and destroy *The God that Failed*.

The 'legion' of ex-communists does not march in close formation. It is scattered far and wide. Its members resemble one another very much, but they also differ. They have common traits and individual features. All have left an army and a camp—some as conscientious objectors, some as deserters, and others as marauders. A few stick quietly to their conscientious objections, while others vociferously claim commissions in an army which they had bitterly opposed. All wear threadbare bits and pieces of the old uniform, supplemented by the quaintest new rags. And all carry with them their common resentments and individual reminiscences.

Some joined the party at one time, others at another; the date of joining is relevant to their further experiences. Those, for instance, who joined in the 1920's went into a movement in which there was plenty of scope for revolutionary idealism. The structure of the party was still fluid; it had not yet gone into the totalitarian mould. Intellectual integrity was still valued in a communist; it had not yet been surrendered for good to Moscow's *raison d'état*. Those who joined the party in the 1930's began their experience on a much lower level. Right from the beginning they were manipulated like recruits on the party's barrack squares by the party's sergeant majors.

This difference bears upon the quality of the ex-communist's reminiscences. Silone, who joined the party in 1921, recalls with real warmth his first contact with it; he conveys fully the intellectual excitement and moral enthusiasm with which communism pulsated in those early days. The reminiscences of Koestler and Spender, who joined in the 1930's, reveal the utter moral and intellectual sterility of the party's first impact on them. Silone and his comrades were intensely concerned with fundamental ideas before and after they became absorbed in the drudgery of day-to-day duty. In Koestler's story, his party 'assignment', right from the first moment, over-shadows all matters of personal conviction and ideal. The communist of the early drafts was a revolutionary before he became, or was expected to become, a puppet. The communist of the later drafts hardly got the chance to breathe the genuine air of revolution.

Nevertheless, the original motives for joining were similar, if not identical, in almost every case: experience of social injustice or degradation; a sense of insecurity bred by slumps and social crises; and the craving for a great ideal or purpose, or for a reliable intellectual guide through the shaky labyrinth of modern society. The new-comer felt the miseries of the old capitalist order to be unbearable; and the glowing light of the Russian revolution illumined those miseries with extraordinary sharp-ness.

Socialism, classless society, the withering away of the State—all seemed around the corner. Few of the new-comers had any premonition of the blood and sweat and tears to come. To himself, the intellectual convert to communism seemed a new Prometheus—except that he would not be pinned to the rock by Zeus's wrath. 'Nothing henceforth [so Koestler now recalls his own mood in those days] can disturb the convert's inner peace and serenity—except the occasional fear of losing faith again. . . .'

Our ex-communist now bitterly denounces the be-trayal of his hopes. This appears to him to have had almost no precedent. Yet as he eloquently describes his early expectations and illusions, we detect a strangely familiar tone. Exactly so did the disillusioned Words-worth and his contemporaries look back upon their first youthful enthusiasm for the French revolution:

> *Bliss was it in that dawn to be alive,*
> *But to be young was very heaven!*

The intellectual communist who breaks away emo-tionally from his party can claim some noble ancestry.

Beethoven tore to pieces the title page of his *Eroica*, on which he had dedicated the symphony to Napoleon, as soon as he learned that the First Consul was about to ascend a throne. Wordsworth called the crowning of Napoleon 'a sad reverse for all mankind'. All over Europe the enthusiasts of the French revolution were stunned by their discovery that the Corsican liberator of the peoples and enemy of tyrants was himself a tyrant and an oppressor.

In the same way the Wordsworths of our days were shocked at the sight of Stalin fraternizing with Hitler and Ribbentrop. If no new *Eroicas* have been created in our days, at least the dedicatory pages of unwritten symphonies have been torn with great flourishes.

In *The God That Failed*, Louis Fischer tries to explain somewhat remorsefully and not quite convincingly why he adhered to the Stalin cult for so long. He analyses the variety of motives, some working slowly and some rapidly, which determine the moment at which people recover from the infatuation with Stalinism. The force of the European disillusionment with Napoleon was almost equally uneven and capricious. A great Italian poet, Ugo Foscolo, who had been Napoleon's soldier and composed an *Ode to Bonaparte the Liberator*, turned against his idol after the Peace of Campoformio—this must have stunned a 'Jacobin' from Venice as the Nazi-Soviet Pact stunned a Polish communist. But a man like Beethoven remained under the spell of Bonaparte for seven years more, until he saw the despot drop his republican mask. This was an 'eye-opener' comparable to Stalin's purge trials of the 1930's.

There can be no greater tragedy than that of a great revolution's succumbing to the mailed fist that was to defend it from its enemies. There can be no spectacle as disgusting as that of a post-revolutionary tyranny dressed up in the banners of liberty. The ex-communist is morally as justified as was the ex-Jacobin in revealing and revolting against that spectacle.

But is it true, as Koestler claims, that 'ex-communists are the only people . . . who know what it's all about'? One may risk the assertion that the exact opposite is true: Of all people, the ex-communists know least what it is all about.

At any rate, the pedagogical pretensions of ex-communist men of letters seem grossly exaggerated. Most of them (Silone is a notable exception) have never been inside the real communist movement, in the thick of its clandestine or open organization. As a rule, they moved on the literary or journalistic fringe of the party. Their notions of communist doctrine and ideology usually spring from their own literary intuition, which is sometimes acute but often misleading.

Worse still is the ex-communist's characteristic incapacity for detachment. His emotional reaction against his former environment keeps him in its deadly grip and prevents him from understanding the drama in which he was involved or half-involved. The picture of communism and Stalinism he draws is that of a gigantic chamber of intellectual and moral horrors. Viewing it, the uninitiated are transferred from politics to pure demonology. Sometimes the artistic effect may be strong —horrors and demons do enter into many a poetic masterpiece; but it is politically unreliable and even dangerous. Of course, the story of Stalinism abounds in horror. But this is only one of its elements; and even this, the demonic, has to be translated into terms of human motives and interests. The ex-communist does not even attempt the translation.

In a rare flash of genuine self-criticism, Koestler makes this admission:

'As a rule, our memories romanticize the past. But when one has renounced a creed or been betrayed by a friend, the opposite mechanism sets to work. In the light of that later knowledge, the original experience loses its innocence, becomes tainted and rancid in recollection. I have tried in these pages to recapture the mood in which the experiences [in the Communist Party] related were originally lived—and I know that I have failed. Irony, anger, and shame kept intruding; the passions of that time seem transformed into perversions, its inner certitude into the closed universe of the drug addict; the shadow of barbed wire lies across the condemned playground of memory. Those who were caught by the great illusion of our time, and have lived through its moral and intellectual debauch, either give themselves up to a new addiction of the opposite type, or are condemned to pay with a lifelong hangover.'

This need not be true of all ex-communists. Some may still feel that their experience has been free from the morbid overtones described by Koestler. Nevertheless, Koestler has given here a truthful and honest characterization of the type of ex-communist to which he himself belongs. But it is difficult to square this self-portrait with his other claim that the confraternity for which he speaks 'are the only people . . . who know what it's all about'. With equal right a sufferer from traumatic shock might claim that he is the only one who really understands wounds and surgery. The most that the intellectual ex-communist knows, or rather feels, is his own sickness; but he is ignorant of the nature of the external violence that has produced it, let alone the cure.

This irrational emotionalism dominates the evolution of many an ex-communist. 'The logic of opposition at all costs', says Silone, 'has carried many ex-communists far from their starting-points, in some cases as far as fascism.' What were those starting-points? Nearly every ex-communist broke with his party in the name of communism. Nearly every one set out to defend the ideal of socialism from the abuses of a bureaucracy subservient to Moscow. Nearly every one began by throwing out the dirty water of the Russian revolution to protect the baby bathing in it.

Sooner or later these intentions are forgotten or abandoned. Having broken with a party bureaucracy in the name of communism, the heretic goes on to break with communism itself. He claims to have made the discovery that the root of the evil goes far deeper than he at first imagined, even though his digging for that 'root' may have been very lazy and very shallow. He no longer defends socialism from unscrupulous abuse; he now defends mankind from the fallacy of socialism. He no longer throws out the dirty water of the Russian revolution to protect the baby; he discovers that the baby is a monster which must be strangled. The heretic becomes a renegade.

How far he departed from his starting-point, whether, as Silone says, he becomes a fascist or not, depends on his inclinations and tastes—and stupid Stalinist heresy-hunting often drives the ex-communist to extremes. But, whatever the shades of individual attitudes, as a rule the intellectual ex-communist ceases to oppose capitalism. Often he rallies to its defence, and he brings to this job the lack of scruple, the narrow-mindedness, the disregard for truth, and the intense hatred with which Stalinism has imbued him. He remains a sectarian. He is an inverted Stalinist. He continues to see the world in white and black, but now the colours are differently distributed. As a communist he saw no difference between fascists and social democrats. As an anti-communist he sees no difference between nazism and communism. Once; he accepted the party's claim to infallibility; now he believes himself to be infallible. Having once been caught by the 'greatest illusion', he is now obsessed by the greatest disillusionment of our time.

His former illusion at least implied a positive ideal. His disillusionment is utterly negative. His role is therefore intellectually and politically barren. In this, too, he resembles the embittered ex-Jacobin of the Napoleonic era. Wordsworth and Coleridge were fatally obsessed with the 'Jacobin danger'; their fear dimmed even their poetic genius. It was Coleridge who denounced in the House of Commons a Bill for the prevention of cruelty to animals as the 'strongest instance of legislative

Jacobinism'. The ex-Jacobin became the prompter of the anti-Jacobin reaction in England. Directly or indirectly, his influence was behind the Bills Against Seditious Writings and Traitorous Correspondence, the Treasonable Practices Bill, and Seditious Meetings Bill (1792–4), the defeats of parliamentary reform, the suspension of the Habeas Corpus Act, and the postponement of the emancipation of England's religious minorities for the lifetime of a generation. Since the conflict with revolutionary France was 'not a time to make hazardous experiments', the slave trade, too, obtained a lease on life—in the name of liberty.

In quite the same way our ex-communist, for the best of reasons, does the most vicious things. He advances bravely in the front rank of every witch hunt. His blind hatred of his former ideal is leaven to contemporary conservatism. Not rarely he denounces even the mildest brand of the 'welfare State' as 'legislative Bolshevism'. He contributes heavily to the moral climate in which a modern counterpart to the English anti-Jacobin reaction is hatched.

His grotesque performance reflects the impasse in which he finds himself. The impasse is not merely his— it is part of a blind alley in which an entire generation leads an incoherent and absent-minded life.

The historical parallel drawn here extends to the wider background of two epochs. The world is split between Stalinism and an anti-Stalinist alliance in much the same way as it was split between Napoleonic France and the Holy Alliance. It is a split between a 'degenerated' revolution exploited by a despot and a grouping of predominantly, although not exclusively, conservative interests. In terms of practical politics the choice seems to be now, as it was then, confined to these alternatives. Yet the rights and the wrongs of this controversy are so hopelessly confused that whichever the choice, and whatever its practical motives, it is almost certain to be wrong in the long run and in the broadest historical sense.

An honest and critically minded man could reconcile himself to Napoleon as little as he can now to Stalin. But despite Napoleon's violence and frauds, the message of the French revolution survived to echo powerfully throughout the nineteenth century. The Holy Alliance freed Europe from Napoleon's oppression; and for a moment its victory was hailed by most Europeans. Yet what Castlereagh and Metternich and Alexander I had to offer to 'liberated' Europe was merely the preservation of an old, decomposing order. Thus the abuses and the aggressiveness of an empire bred by the revolution gave a new lease on life to European feudalism. This was the ex-Jacobin's most unexpected triumph. But the price he paid for it was that presently he himself, and his anti-Jacobin cause, looked like vicious, ridiculous anachronisms. In the year of Napoleon's defeat, Shelley wrote to Wordsworth:

> *In honoured poverty thy voice did weave*
> *Songs consecrate to truth and liberty—*
> *Deserting these, thou leavest me to grieve,*
> *Thus having been, that thou shouldst cease to be.*

If our ex-communist had any historical sense, he would ponder this lesson.

Some of the ex-Jacobin prompters of the anti-Jacobin reaction had as few scruples about their *volte-face* as have the Burnhams and the Ruth Fischers of our days. Others were remorseful, and pleaded patriotic sentiment, or a philosophy of the lesser evil, or both, to explain why they had sided with old dynasties against an upstart emperor. If they did not deny the vices of the Courts and the governments they had once denounced, they claimed that those governments were more liberal than Napoleon. This was certainly true of Pitt's government, even though in the long run the social and political influence of Napoleonic France on European civilization was more permanent and fruitful than that of Pitt's England, not to speak of the influence of Metternich's Austria or Alexander's Russia. 'O grief that Earth's best hopes rest all in thee!'—this was the sigh of resignation with which Wordsworth reconciled himself to Pitt's England. 'Far, far more abject is thy enemy' was his formula of reconciliation.

'Far, far more abject is thy enemy' might have been the text for *The God That Failed*, and for the philosophy of the lesser evil expounded in its pages. The ardour with which the writers of this book defend the West against Russia and communism is sometimes chilled by uncertainty or residual ideological inhibition. The uncertainty appears between the lines of their confessions, or in curious asides.

Silone, for instance, still describes the pre-Mussolini Italy, against which, as a communist, he had rebelled, as 'pseudo-democratic'. He hardly believes that post-Mussolini Italy is any better, but he sees its Stalinist enemy to be 'far, far more abject'. More than the other co-authors of this book, Silone is surely aware of the price that Europeans of his generation have already paid for the acceptance of lesser-evil philosophies. Louis Fischer advocates the 'double rejection' of communism and capitalism, but his rejection of the latter sounds like a feeble face-saving formula; and his newly found cult of Gandhiism impresses one as merely an awkward escapism. But it is Koestler who, occasionally, in the midst of all his affectation and anti-communist frenzy, reveals a few curious mental reservations: '. . . if we survey history [he says] and compare the lofty aims, in the name of which revolutions were started, and the sorry end to which they came, we see again and again how a *polluted civilization pollutes its own revolutionary offspring*' (my italics). Has Koestler thought out the implications of his own words, or is he merely throwing out a *bon mot*? If the 'revolutionary offspring', communism, has really been 'polluted' by the civilization against which it has rebelled, then no matter how repulsive the offspring may be, the source of the evil is not in it but in that civilization. And this will be so regardless of how zealously Koestler himself may act as the advocate of the 'defenders' of civilization *à la* Chambers.

Even more startling is another thought—or is this perhaps also only a *bon mot*?—with which Koestler unexpectedly ends his confession:

'I served the Communist Party for seven years—the same length of time as Jacob tended Laban's sheep to win Rachel his daughter. When the time was up, the bride was led into his dark tent; only the next morning did he discover that his ardours had been spent not on the lovely Rachel but on the ugly Leah.

'I wonder whether he ever recovered from the shock of having slept with an illusion. I wonder whether afterwards he believed that he had ever believed in it. I wonder whether the happy end of the legend will be repeated; for at the price of another seven years of labour, Jacob was given Rachel too, and the illusion became flesh.

'And the seven years seemed unto him but a few days, for the love he had for her.'

One might think that Jacob-Koestler reflects uneasily whether he has not too hastily ceased tending Laban-Stalin's sheep, instead of waiting patiently till his 'illusion became flesh'.

The words are not meant to blame, let alone to castigate, anybody. Their purpose, let this be repeated, is to throw into relief a confusion of ideas, from which the ex-communist intellectual is not the only sufferer.

In one of his recent articles, Koestler vented his irritation at those good old liberals who were shocked by the excess of anti-communist zeal in the former communist, and viewed him with the disgust with which ordinary people look at 'a defrocked priest taking out a girl to a dance'.

Well, the good old liberals may be right, after all: this peculiar type of anti-communist may appear to them like a defrocked priest 'taking out', not just a girl, but a harlot. The ex-communist's utter confusion of intellect and emotion makes him ill-suited for any political activity. He is haunted by a vague sense that he has betrayed either his former ideals or the ideals of bourgeois society; like Koestler, he may even have an ambivalent notion that he has betrayed both. He then tries to suppress his sense of guilt and uncertainty, or to camouflage it by a show of extraordinary certitude and frantic aggressiveness. He insists that the world should recognize his uneasy conscience as the clearest conscience of all. He may no longer be concerned with any cause except one—self-justification. And this is the most dangerous motive for any political activity.

It seems that the only dignified attitude the intellectual ex-communist can take is to rise *au-dessus de la mêlée*. He cannot join the Stalinist camp or the anti-Stalinist Holy Alliance without doing violence to his better self. So let him stay outside any camp. Let him try to regain critical sense and intellectual detachment. Let him overcome the cheap ambition to have a finger in the political pie. Let him be at peace with his own self at least, if the price he has to pay for a phony peace with the world is self-renunciation and self-denunciation.

This is not to say that the ex-communist man of letters, or intellectual at large, should retire into the ivory tower. (His contempt for the ivory tower lingers in him from his past.) But he may withdraw into a *watch-tower* instead. To watch with detachment and alertness this heaving chaos of a world, to be on a sharp lookout for what is going to emerge from it, and to interpret it *sine ira et studio*—this is now the only honourable service the ex-communist intellectual can render to a generation in which scrupulous observation and honest interpretation have become so sadly rare. (Is it not striking how little observation and interpretation, and how much philosophizing and sermonizing, one finds in the books of the gifted pleiad of ex-communist writers?)

But can the intellectual really now be a detached observer of this world? Even if taking sides makes him identify himself with causes that, in truth, are not his, must he not takes sides all the same? Well, we can recall some great 'intellectuals' who, in a similar situation in the past, refused to identify themselves with any established Cause. Their attitude seemed incomprehensible to many of their contemporaries: but history has proved their judgment to have been superior to the phobias and hatreds of their age. Three names may be mentioned here: Jefferson, Goethe, and Shelley. All three, each in a different way, were confronted with the choice between the Napoleonic idea and the Holy Alliance. All three, again each in a different manner, refused to choose.

Jefferson was the staunchest friend of the French revolution in its early heroic period. He was willing to forgive even the Terror, but he turned away in disgust from Napoleon's 'military despotism'. Yet he had no truck with Bonaparte's enemies, Europe's 'hypocritical deliverers', as he called them. His detachment was not merely suited to the diplomatic interest of a young and neutral republic; it resulted naturally from his republican conviction and democratic passion.

Unlike Jefferson, Goethe lived right inside the storm centre. Napoleon's troops and Alexander's soldiers, in turn, took up quarters in his Weimar. As the Minister of his Prince, Goethe opportunistically bowed to every invader. But as a thinker and man, he remained noncommittal and aloof. He was aware of the grandeur of the French revolution and was shocked by its horrors. He greeted the sound of French guns at Valmy as the opening of a new and better epoch, and he saw through Napoleon's follies. He acclaimed the liberation of Germany from Napoleon, and he was acutely aware of the misery of that 'liberation'. His aloofness, in these as in other matters, gained him the reputation of 'the Olympian'; and the label was not always meant to be flattering. But his Olympian appearance was due least of all to an inner indifference to the fate of his contemporaries. It veiled his drama: his incapacity and reluctance to identify himself with causes, each an inextricable tangle of right and wrong.

Finally, Shelley watched the clash of the two worlds with all the burning passion, anger, and hope of which his great young soul was capable: he surely was no Olympian. Yet, not for a single moment did he accept the self-righteous claims and pretensions of any of the belligerents. Unlike the ex-Jacobins, who were older than he, he was true to the Jacobin republican idea. It was as a republican, and not as a patriot of the England of George III, that he greeted the fall of Napoleon, that 'most unambitious slave' who did 'dance and revel on the grave of Liberty'. But as a republican he knew also that 'virtue owns a more eternal foe' than Bonapartist force and fraud—'old Custom, legal Crime, and bloody Faith' embodied in the Holy Alliance.

All three—Jefferson, Goethe, and Shelley—were in a sense outsiders to the great conflict of their time, and because of this they interpreted their time with more truthfulness and penetration than did the fearful—the hateridden partisans on either side.

What a pity and what a shame it is that most ex-communist intellectuals are inclined to follow the tradition of Wordsworth and Coleridge rather than that of Goethe and Shelley.

THE TRAGIC LIFE
OF A POLRUGARIAN MINISTER[1]

POLRUGARIA need not be exactly located on the map.
Enough that it lies somewhere in the eastern reaches
of Europe. Nor need the name of Vincent Adriano, a
high Polrugarian official, be looked up in any *Who's
Who*, for he is a half-real and half-imaginary character.
Adriano's features and traits can be found in some of the
people who now rule the Russian satellite countries, and
not a single one of his experiences related here has been
invented. It need not be specified what post Vincent
Adriano holds in his government. He may be the Presi-
dent or the Prime Minister or the Vice-Premier, or he
may be only the Minister of the Interior or the Minister
of Education. In all likelihood he is a member of the
Politbureau, and is known as one of the pillars of the
People's Democracy in Polrugaria. His words and doings
are reported in newspapers all over the world.

It is common to refer to men of Adriano's kind as
'Stalin's henchmen', 'Russian puppets', and 'leaders of
the Cominform fifth column'. If any of these labels described him adequately, Adriano would not be worth any
special attention. To be sure, he is unavoidably something of a puppet and an agent of a foreign power, but he
is much more than that.

Vincent Adriano is in either his late forties or early
fifties—he may be just fifty. His age is significant because
his formative years were those of the revolutionary aftermath of the First World War. He came from a middle-
class family that before 1914 had enjoyed a measure of

[1] Written in 1950.

23

prosperity and believed in the stability of dynasties, governments, currencies, and moral principles. In his middle or late teens, Adriano saw three vast empires crumble with hardly anybody shedding a tear. Then he watched many governments leap into and tumble out of existence in so rapid and breathtaking a succession that it was almost impossible to keep account of them. On the average, there were a dozen or a score of them every year. The advent of each was hailed as an epoch-making event; each successive Prime Minister was greeted as a saviour. After a few weeks or days, he was booed and hissed out of office as a misfit, scoundrel, and nincompoop.

The currency of Polrugaria, like the currencies of all neighbouring countries, lost its value from month to month, then from day to day, and finally from hour to hour. Adriano's father sold his house at the beginning of one year; with the money he received he could buy only two boxes of matches at the end of that year. No political combination, no institution, no established custom, no inherited idea seemed capable of survival. Moral principles, too, were in flux. Reality seemed to lose clear-cut outline, and this was reflected in the new poetry, painting, and sculpture.

The young man was easily convinced that he was witnessing the decay of a social order, that before his very eyes capitalism was succumbing to the attack of its own deep-seated insanity. He was aroused by the fiery manifestos of the Communist International signed by Lenin and Trotsky. Soon he became a member of the Communist Party. Since in Polrugaria the party was savagely persecuted—the penalties for membership ranged from five years' imprisonment to death—the people who joined it did not do so, in those days, for selfish or careerist motives.

Adriano, at any rate, gave up without hesitation the prospect of a secure career in the academic field to become a professional revolutionary. He was prompted by idealistic sympathy with the underdog and by something he called 'scientific conviction'. Studying the classics of Marxism, he became firmly convinced that private ownership of the means of production and the concept of the nation-state had outlived their day, and further, that they were certain to be replaced by an international socialist society which could be promoted only by a proletarian dictatorship.

Proletarian dictatorship meant not the dictatorial rule of a clique, let alone of a single leader, but the social and political predominance of the working classes, 'the dictatorship of an overwhelming majority of the people over a handful of exploiters, semi-feudal landlords, and big capitalists'. Far from disowning democracy, the proletarian dictatorship, so he thought, would represent its consummation. It would fill the empty shell of formal equality, which was all that bourgeois democracy could offer, with the content of social equality. With this vision of the future he plunged deep into the revolutionary underground.

We need not relate in detail Adriano's revolutionary career—its pattern was, up to a point, typical. There were the years of his dangerous work in the underground, when he lived the life of a hunted man without name or address. He organized strikes, wrote for clandestine papers, and travelled all over the country studying social conditions and setting up organizations. Then came the years of prison and torture and of longing in solitude. The vision of the future that had inspired him had to be somewhat adulterated with expedients, tactical games, and tricks of organization—the daily business of every politician, even of one who serves a revolution. For all that, his idealism and enthusiasm had not yet begun to evaporate.

Even while imprisoned he helped sustain in his comrades their conviction, their hope, and their pride in their own sacrifices. Once he led several hundred political prisoners in a hunger strike. The strike, lasting six or seven weeks, was one of the longest ever known. The governor of the prison knew that in order to break it he had first to break Vincent Adriano. Guards dragged the emaciated man by his legs from a cell on the sixth floor down the iron staircase, banging his head against the hard and rusty edges of the steps until he lost consciousness. Vincent Adriano became a legendary hero.

With some of his comrades, he at last managed to escape from prison and make his way to Russia. Inasmuch as he spent several years in Moscow, it is now often said and written about him that he belongs to that 'hard core of Moscow-trained agents who control Polrugaria'. Such words, when he happens to read them, bring a sadly ironical smile to his lips.

When Adriano arrived in Moscow in the early 1930's, he was not among the chief leaders of the Polrugarian party. Nor was he greatly concerned with his place in the hierarchy. He was more preoccupied with the confusion in his own mind that arose when he first compared his vision of the society of the future with life in the Soviet Union under Stalin. He hardly dared admit, even to himself, the extent of his disillusionment. This, too, has been so typical in the experiences of men of his kind that we need not dwell on it. Typical, too, were the truisms, the half-truths, and the self-delusions with which he tried to soothe his disturbed communist conscience. Russia's inherited poverty, her isolation in a capitalist world, the dangers threatening her from outside, the illiteracy of her masses, their laziness and lack of civic responsibility—all this and more he evoked to explain to himself why life in Russia fell appallingly short of the ideal.

'Oh,' he sighed, 'if only the revolution had first been victorious in a more civilized and advanced country! But history has to be taken as it is, and Russia is at least entitled to the respect and gratitude due the pioneer, whatever that pioneer's faults and vices.' He did his utmost not to see the realities of life around him.

Then came the great purges of 1936–8. Most leaders of the Polrugarian party who had lived as exiles in Moscow were shot as spies, saboteurs, and agents of the Polrugarian political police. Before they died, they (and even their wives, brothers, and sisters) were made to bear witness against one another. Among the dishonoured and the executed was one who more than anybody else had aroused Adriano's enthusiasm and sustained his courage, who had initiated him into the most difficult problems of Marxist theory, and to whom Adriano had looked up as a friend and spiritual guide.

Adriano, too, was confronted with the usual charges. By a freak of fortune, however, or perhaps by the whim of the chief of the G.P.U., Yezhov, or of one of Yezhov's underlings, he was not made to face a firing-squad. Instead, he was deported to a forced-labour camp somewhere in the subpolar north. With many others—Trotskyites, Zinovievites, Bukharinites, kulaks, Ukrainian nationalists, bandits and thieves, former generals, former university professors and party organizers— he was employed in felling trees and transporting them from a forest to a depot. Frost, hunger, and disease took their toll of the deportees, but the ranks were constantly filled with newcomers.

Adriano saw how people around him were first reduced to an animal-like struggle for survival, how they next lost the will to struggle and survive, and how finally they collapsed and died like flies. Somehow his own vitality did not sag. He went on wielding the axe with his frostbitten fingers. Every third or fourth day it was his turn to harness himself, along with fellow prisoners, to the cart loaded with timber and to drag it across the snow- and ice-covered plain to the depot several miles away. Those were the worst hours. He could not reconcile himself to the fact that he, the proud revolutionary, was being used as a beast of burden in the country of his dream.

Even now he still feels a piercing pain in his heart

whenever he thinks of those days—and that is why he reads with a melancholy smile the stories about the mysterious 'training in fifth-column activity' he received in Russia.

With a shred of his mind he tried to penetrate the tangle of circumstances behind his extraordinary degradation. At night he argued about this with the other deportees. The problem was vast and confused beyond comprehension. Some of the deported communists said that Stalin had carried out a counter-revolution in which every achievement of Lenin's revolution had been destroyed.

Others held that the foundations of the revolution—public ownership and a collectivist economy—had remained intact, but that instead of a free socialist society, a terrifying combination of socialism and slavery was being erected on those foundations. The outlook was therefore more difficult than anything they could have imagined, but there was perhaps some hope, if not for this generation then for the next. Stalinism, it was true, was casting grave discredit upon the ideal of socialism, but perhaps what was left of socialism might still be salvaged from the wreckage. Adriano could not quite make up his mind, but he was inclined to adopt this latter view.

Events now took a turn so fantastic that even the most fertile imagination could not have conceived it. One day, towards the end of 1941 (Hitler's armies had just been repulsed from the gates of the Russian capital), Adriano was freed from the concentration camp and taken with great honours straight to Moscow. The Kremlin urgently needed East and Central European communists capable of broadcasting to the Nazi-occupied lands and of establishing liaison with the underground movements behind the enemy lines. Because of their country's strategic importance, Polrugarians were especially wanted. But not a single one of the chief leaders of the Polrugarian party was alive. The few less prominent ones who had been dispersed in various places of deportation were hurriedly brought back to Moscow, rehabilitated, and put to work. The rehabilitation took the form of an apology from the Security Police to the effect that the deportation of Comrade So-and-So had been a regrettable mistake.

Several times a week, Adriano, facing the microphone, shouted into the ether his confidence in the Land of Socialism, extolled Stalin and his achievements, and called on the Polrugarians to rise behind the enemy lines and prepare for liberation.

He sensed sharply the incongruity of his situation. He was now a propaganda agent for his jailers and torturers, for those who had denigrated and destroyed the leaders of Polrugarian communism, his friend and guide among them. At heart he could neither forget nor forgive the agony and the shame of the purges. And with a part of his mind he could never detach himself from the people he had left behind in the north.

But he could not refuse the assignment. Refusal would have amounted to sabotage of the war effort, and the penalty would have been death or deportation. Yet it was not merely for life's sake that he was doing his job. He was eager to help defeat the Nazis, and for this, he felt, it was right to join hands 'with the devil and his grandmother'—and with Stalin.

Nor was this merely a matter of defeating Nazism. Despite all he had gone through, he clung to his old ideas and hopes. He was still a communist. He looked forward to the revolutionary ferment that would spread over the capitalist world after the war. The more severe his disillusionment with the Soviet Union, the more intense was his hope that the victory of communism in other countries would regenerate the movement and free it from the Kremlin's faithless tutelage.

The same motives prompted him to agree to a proposal, which Stalin personally made to him a few months later, that he should organize a Polrugarian Committee of

Liberation and become its secretary. It was certain that the Red Army would cross into Polrugaria sooner or later. The Committee of Liberation was to follow in its wake and to become the nucleus of a provisional government.

Adriano's hands were full of work. He was now in charge of liaison with the Polrugarian Resistance. He issued instructions to the emissaries who penetrated the enemy lines or were parachuted behind them. He received reports from the guerrillas in the occupied country and transmitted them higher up. He arranged that leaders of the non-communist and even anti-communist parties be smuggled out of the country and brought to Moscow. And he induced some of them to join the Committee of Liberation.

The sequel is known. The Committee of Liberation became the provisional government, and then the actual government of Polrugaria. The non-communist parties were squeezed out one by one and suppressed. Polrugaria became a People's Democracy. Adriano is one of the pillars of the new government, and so far nothing seems to foreshadow his eclipse. He has not found the way out of the trap; neither has he been crushed in it.

There are two Vincent Adrianos now. One seems never to have known a moment of doubt or hesitation. His Stalinist orthodoxy has never been questioned, his devotion to the party has never flagged, and his virtues as leader and statesman are held to be unsurpassed. The other Adriano is almost constantly tormented by his communist conscience, a prey to scruple and fear, to illusion and disillusionment. The former is expansive and eloquent, the latter broods in silence and hides even from his oldest friends. The former acts, the latter never ceases to ponder.

From 1945 to 1947 the two Adrianos were almost reconciled with each other. In those years the Polrugarian party carried out some of the root-and-branch

reforms that for decades had been inscribed in its programme. It attacked the problem of Polrugarian land-
lordism. It divided the large semi-feudal estates among
the land-hungry peasants. It established public ownership of large-scale industry. It initiated impressive plans
for the further industrial development of a sadly underdeveloped country. It sponsored a great deal of progressive social legislation and an ambitious educational
reform. These achievements filled Adriano with real joy
and pride. It was, after all, for these things that he had
languished in Polrugarian prisons.

In those years, too, Moscow, for its own reasons, was
telling the Polrugarians that they should not look too
much to Russia as their model, that they ought to find
and follow their own 'Polrugarian road to socialism'. To
Adriano this meant that Polrugaria would be spared the
experience of purges and concentration camps, of abject
subservience and fear. Communism, intense industrial
and educational development, and a measure of real freedom to argue with one's fellow and to criticize the
powers that be—this seemed to be the achievement of an
ideal.

What disturbed him even then was that the people of
Polrugaria were showing little enthusiasm for the revolution. To be sure, they saw the advantages and on the
whole approved them. But they resented the revolution
that was being carried out over their heads by people
whom they had not chosen and who did not often bother
to consult them and who looked like stooges of a foreign
power.

Adriano knew to what extent the presence of the Red
Army in Polrugaria had facilitated the revolution. Without it, the forces of the counter-revolution, with the
assistance of the Western bourgeois democracies, might
have reasserted themselves in bloody civil war, as they
had done after the First World War. But he reflected
that a revolution without genuine popular enthusiasm
behind it is half defeated. It is inclined to distrust the

people whom it should serve. And distrust may breed dark fear and terror as it had done in Russia.

Yet, although he saw these dangers, he hoped that through honest and devoted work for the masses, the new Polrugarian government could eventually win their confidence and arouse their enthusiasm. Then the new social order would stand on its own feet. Sooner or later the Russian armies would go back to Russia. Surely, he thought, there must be another road to socialism, perhaps not exactly a Polrugarian one, but not a Russian and a Stalinist road either.

In the meantime, Vincent Adriano did a few things that were understood only by the initiated. He sponsored in Polrugaria a cult to glorify the memory of his old friend and guide who had perished in Russia, although Moscow had not officially rehabilitated the latter's memory. The biography of the dead leader can even now be seen displayed in Polrugarian bookshops, side by side with the official life of Stalin. Since the circumstances of the martyr's death are not mentioned in the biography, only the older communists are aware of the hidden implications of this homage.

Adriano has also set up a special institute which looks after the families of all the Polrugarian communists who perished in Moscow as 'spies and traitors'. The institute is called the Foundation of the Veterans and Martyrs of the Revolution. Such gestures give Adriano a measure of moral satisfaction, but he knows that politically they are irrelevant.

As the two camps, East and West, began to marshal their forces and as the leaders on both sides, each in their own ways, confronted everybody with a categorical 'who-is-not-with-me-is-against-me', Adriano's prospects darkened. If he could have had his way, Adriano's answer would have been a hearty 'plague o' both your houses'. He who has been an outcast in Stalin's Russia, a beast of burden in one of his concentration camps, he to whom every copy of *Pravda*, with its demented hymns to Stalin, gives an acute sensation of nausea, has watched with a shudder as his 'Polrugarian road to socialism' has become more and more the Stalinist road. Yet he does not see how he can depart from it.

He takes it for granted that all the West can offer to East and Central Europe is counter-revolution. The West may extol freedom and the dignity of man (and who has explored the meaning of these ideals as tragically and thoroughly as Adriano?), but his gaze is fixed on the gulf he sees between Western promise and fulfilment. He is convinced that in his part of the world every new upheaval will bring more rather than less oppression, more rather than less degradation of man.

He is willing to concede that those who speak for the West may be quite sincere in their promises, but he adds that he has retained his old Marxist habit of disregarding the wishes and promises of statesmen and of keeping his eyes on social and political realities. Who among the Polrugarians, he asks, are ready to rally to the banners of the West? There may be a few well-meaning people among them, but these will be the dupes.

The most active and energetic allies of the West in Polrugaria are those who have had a stake in the old social order, the privileged men of the pre-war dictatorship, the old *soldateska*, the expropriated landlords and their like. These, should the West win, will form the new government, and, in the name of freedom and of the dignity of man, let loose a White terror the like of which has never been seen. Adriano had known *their* terror once, also. But that was at a time when the old ruling class believed that their rule would last for ever, and when their self-confidence prevented their terror from becoming altogether insane. Now, if they came back, they would be mad with fear and revenge. The real choice, as he sees it, is not between tyranny and freedom, but between Stalinist tyranny, which is in part redeemed by economic and social progress, and a reactionary tyranny which would not be redeemed by anything.

At times Adriano would be happy to give up his high office and withdraw into obscurity. But the world has become too small. He cannot seek asylum in the West. This, in his eyes, would be not much better than treason —not to Russia, but to his ideal of communism. Nor can he withdraw into obscurity. Resignation and withdrawal on his part would be a gesture of opposition and defiance, and this the régime he has helped to build would not allow.

How much is there in common between the young man who once set out with Promethean ardour to conquer history's insanity as it manifested itself in capitalism and the middle-aged Cabinet Minister who vaguely feels that history's irrational forces have overpowered the camp of the revolution, too, and, incidentally, driven him into a trap? He does his best to bolster his own self-respect and to persuade himself that as statesman, dignitary, and leader he is still the same man he was when he championed the cause of the oppressed and suffered for it in the prisons of his native land. But sometimes, while he solemnly receives delegations of peasants or salutes a colourful parade, a familiar sharp pain pierces his heart; and suddenly he feels that he is merely a pathetic wreck, a subpolar beast of burden.

'1984'—THE MYSTICISM OF CRUELTY[1]

Few novels written in this generation have obtained a popularity as great as that of George Orwell's *1984*. Few, if any, have made a similar impact on politics. The title of Orwell's book is a political by-word. The terms coined by him—'Newspeak', 'Oldspeak', 'Mutability of the Past', 'Big Brother', 'Ministry of Truth', 'Thought Police', 'Crimethink', 'Doublethink', 'Hateweek', etc.—have entered the political vocabulary; they occur in most newspaper articles and speeches denouncing Russia and communism. Television and the cinema have familiarized many millions of viewers on both sides of the Atlantic with the menacing face of Big Brother and the nightmare of a supposedly communist Oceania. The novel has served as a sort of an ideological super-weapon in the cold war. As in no other book or document, the convulsive fear of communism, which has swept the West since the end of the Second World War, has been reflected and focused in *1984*.

The cold war has created a 'social demand' for such an ideological weapon just as it creates the demand for physical super-weapons. But the super-weapons are genuine feats of technology; and there can be no discrepancy between the uses to which they may be put and the intention of their producers: they are meant to spread death or at least to threaten utter destruction. A book like *1984* may be used without much regard for the author's intention. Some of its features may be torn out of their context, while others, which do not suit the poli-

[1] Written in December 1954.

35

tical purpose which the book is made to serve, are ignored or virtually suppressed. Nor need a book like *1984* be a literary masterpiece or even an important and original work to make its impact. Indeed a work of great literary merit is usually too rich in its texture and too subtle in thought and form to lend itself to adventitious exploitation. As a rule, its symbols cannot easily be transformed into hypnotizing bogies, or its ideas turned into slogans. The words of a great poet when they enter the political vocabulary do so by a process of slow, almost imperceptible infiltration, not by a frantic incursion. The literary masterpiece influences the political mind by fertilizing and enriching it from the inside, not by stunning it.

1984 is the work of an intense and concentrated, but also fear-ridden and restricted imagination. A hostile critic has dismissed it as a 'political horror-comic'. This is not a fair description: there are in Orwell's novel certain layers of thought and feeling which raise it well above that level. But it is a fact that the symbolism of *1984* is crude; that its chief symbol, Big Brother, resembles the bogy-man of a rather inartistic nursery tale; and that Orwell's story unfolds like the plot of a science-fiction film of the cheaper variety, with mechanical horror piling up upon mechanical horror so much that, in the end, Orwell's subtler ideas, his pity for his characters, and his satire on the society of his own days (not of 1984) may fail to communicate themselves to the reader. *1984* does not seem to justify the description of Orwell as the modern Swift, a description for which *Animal Farm* provides some justification. Orwell lacks the richness and subtlety of thought and the philosophical detachment of the great satirist. His imagination is ferocious and at times penetrating, but it lacks width, suppleness, and originality.

The lack of originality is illustrated by the fact that Orwell borrowed the idea of *1984*, the plot, the chief characters, the symbols, and the whole climate of his story from a Russian writer who has remained almost unknown in the West. That writer is Evgenii Zamyatin, and the title of the book which served Orwell as the model is *We*. Like *1984*, *We* is an 'anti-Utopia', a nightmare vision of the shape of things to come, and a Cassandra cry. Orwell's work is a thoroughly English variation on Zamyatin's theme; and it is perhaps only the thoroughness of Orwell's English approach that gives to his work the originality that it possesses.

A few words about Zamyatin may not be out of place here: there are some points of resemblance in the life stories of the two writers. Zamyatin belonged to an older generation: he was born in 1884 and died in 1937. His early writings, like some of Orwell's, were realistic descriptions of the lower middle class. In his experience the Russian revolution of 1905 played approximately the same role that the Spanish civil war played in Orwell's. He participated in the revolutionary movement, was a member of the Russian Social Democratic Party (to which Bolsheviks and Mensheviks then still belonged), and was persecuted by the Tsarist police. At the ebb of the revolution, he succumbed to a mood of 'cosmic pessimism'; and he severed his connection with the Socialist Party, a thing which Orwell, less consistent and to the end influenced by a lingering loyalty to socialism, did not do. In 1917 Zamyatin viewed the new revolution with cold and disillusioned eyes, convinced that nothing good would come out of it. After a brief imprisonment, he was allowed by the Bolshevik government to go abroad; and it was as an émigré in Paris that he wrote *We* in the early 1920's.

The assertion that Orwell borrowed the main elements of *1984* from Zamyatin is not the guess of a critic with a foible for tracing literary influences. Orwell knew Zamyatin's novel and was fascinated by it. He wrote an essay about it, which appeared in the left-socialist *Tribune*, of which Orwell was Literary Editor, on 4 January 1946, just after the publication of *Animal Farm* and before he began writing *1984*. The essay is remarkable not only as

a conclusive piece of evidence, supplied by Orwell himself, on the origin of *1984*, but also as a commentary on
the idea underlying both *We* and *1984*.

The essay begins with Orwell saying that after having
for years looked in vain for Zamyatin's novel, he had at
last obtained it in a French edition (under the title
Nous Autres), and that he was surprised that it had not
been published in England, although an American edition had appeared without arousing much interest. 'So
far as I can judge', Orwell went on, 'it is not a book of
the first order, but it is certainly an unusual one, and it is
astonishing that no English publisher has been enter-
prising enough to re-issue it.' (He concluded the essay
with the words: 'This is a book to look out for when an
English version appears.')

Orwell noticed that Aldous Huxley's *Brave New World*
'must be partly derived' from Zamyatin's novel and
wondered why this had 'never been pointed out'.
Zamyatin's book was, in his view, much superior and
more 'relevant to our own situation' than Huxley's. It
dealt 'with the rebellion of the primitive human spirit
against a rationalized, mechanized, painless world'.

'Painless' is not the right adjective: the world of
Zamyatin's vision is as full of horrors as is that of *1984*.
Orwell himself produced in his essay a succinct cata-
logue of those horrors so that his essay reads now like a
synopsis of *1984*. The members of the society described
by Zamyatin, says Orwell, 'have so completely lost their
individuality as to be known only by numbers. They
live in glass houses . . . which enables the political police,
known as the "Guardians", to supervise them more
easily. They all wear identical uniforms, and a human
being is commonly referred to either as "a number" or
a "unif" (uniform).' Orwell remarks in parenthesis that
Zamyatin wrote 'before television was invented'. In
1984 this technological refinement is brought in as well
as the helicopters from which the police supervise the
homes of the citizens of Oceania in the opening passages

of the novel. The 'unifs' suggest the 'Proles'. In Zamyatin's society of the future as in *1984* love is forbidden:
sexual intercourse is strictly rationed and permitted only
as an unemotional act. 'The Single State is ruled over by
a person known as the Benefactor', the obvious prototype of Big Brother.

'The guiding principle of the State is that happiness
and freedom are incompatible . . . the Single State has
restored his [man's] happiness by removing his freedom.' Orwell describes Zamyatin's chief character as 'a
sort of Utopian Billy Brown of London town' who is
'constantly horrified by the atavistic impulses which
seize upon him'. In Orwell's novel that Utopian Billy
Brown is christened Winston Smith, and his problem
is the same.

For the main *motif* of his plot Orwell is similarly indebted to the Russian writer. This is how Orwell defines
it: 'In spite of education and the vigilance of the
Guardians, many of the ancient human instincts are still
there.' Zamyatin's chief character 'falls in love (this is a
crime, of course) with a certain I-330' just as Winston
Smith commits the crime of falling in love with Julia.
In Zamyatin's as in Orwell's story the love affair is
mixed up with the hero's participation in an 'underground resistance movement'. Zamyatin's rebels 'apart
from plotting the overthrow of the State, even indulge,
at the moment when their curtains are down, in such
vices as smoking cigarettes and drinking alcohol';
Winston Smith and Julia indulge in drinking 'real
coffee with real sugar' in their hideout over Mr.
Charrington's shop. In both novels the crime and the
conspiracy are, of course, discovered by the Guardians
or the Thought Police; and in both the hero 'is ultimately saved from the consequences of his own folly'.

The combination of 'cure' and torture by which
Zamyatin's and Orwell's rebels are 'freed' from the
atavistic impulses, until they begin to love Benefactor
or Big Brother, are very much the same. In Zamyatin:

'The authorities announce that they have discovered the cause of the recent disorders: it is that some human beings suffer from a disease called imagination. The nerve centre responsible for imagination has now been located, and the disease can be cured by X-ray treatment. D-503 undergoes the operation, after which it is easy for him to do what he has known all along that he ought to do—that is, betray his confederates to the police.' In both novels the act of confession and the betrayal of the woman the hero loves are the curative shocks.

Orwell quotes the following scene of torture from Zamyatin:

'She looked at me, her hands clasping the arms of the chair, until her eyes were completely shut. They took her out, brought her to herself by means of an electric shock, and put her under the bell again. This operation was repeated three times, and not a word issued from her lips.'

In Orwell's scenes of torture the 'electric shocks' and the 'arms of the chair' recur quite often, but Orwell is far more intense, masochistic-sadistic, in his descriptions of cruelty and pain. For instance:

'Without any warning except a slight movement of O'Brien's hand, a wave of pain flooded his body. It was a frightening pain, because he could not see what was happening, and he had the feeling that some mortal injury was being done to him. He did not know whether the thing was really happening, or whether the effect was electrically produced; but his body had been wrenched out of shape, the joints were being slowly torn apart. Although the pain had brought the sweat out on his forehead, the worst of all was the fear that his backbone was about to snap. He set his teeth and breathed hard through his nose, trying to keep silent as long as possible.'

The list of Orwell's borrowings is far from complete; but let us now turn from the plot of the two novels to

their underlying idea. Taking up the comparison between Zamyatin and Huxley, Orwell says: 'It is this
intuitive grasp of the irrational side of totalitarianism—
human sacrifice, cruelty as an end in itself, the worship
of a Leader who is credited with divine attributes—that
makes Zamyatin's book superior to Huxley's.' It is this,
we may add, that made of it Orwell's model. Criticizing Huxley, Orwell writes that he could find no clear
reason why the society of *Brave New World* should be
so rigidly and elaborately stratified: 'The aim is not
economic exploitation. . . . *There is no power-hunger, no
sadism, no hardness of any kind.* Those at the top have
no strong motive for staying on the top, and though
everyone is happy in a vacuous way, life has become so
pointless that it is difficult to believe that such a society
could endure.' (My italics.) In contrast, the society of
Zamyatin's anti-Utopia could endure, in Orwell's view,
because in it the supreme motive of action and the reason
for social stratification are not economic exploitation,
for which there is no need, but precisely the 'power-
hunger, sadism, and hardness' of those who 'stay at
the top'. It is easy to recognize in this the *leitmotif* of
1984.

In Oceania technological development has reached so
high a level that society could well satisfy all its material
needs and establish equality in its midst. But inequality
and poverty are maintained in order to keep Big Brother
in power. In the past, says Orwell, dictatorship safe-
guarded inequality, now inequality safeguards dictatorship. But what purpose does the dictatorship itself serve?
'The party seeks power entirely for its own sake. . . .
Power is not a means, it is an end. One does not establish a dictatorship in order to safeguard a revolution;
one makes the revolution in order to establish the dictatorship. The object of persecution is persecution. . . .
The object of power is power.'

Orwell wondered whether Zamyatin did 'intend the
Soviet régime to be the special target of his satire'. He

was not sure of this: 'What Zamyatin seems to be aiming at is not any particular country but the implied aims of the industrial civilization. . . . It is evident from *We* that he had a strong leaning towards primitivism. . . . *We* is in effect a study of the Machine, the genie that man has thoughtlessly let out of its bottle and cannot put back again.' The same ambiguity of the author's aim is evident also in *1984*.

Orwell's guess about Zamyatin was correct. Though Zamyatin was opposed to the Soviet régime, it was not exclusively, or even mainly, that régime which he satirized. As Orwell rightly remarked, the early Soviet Russia had few features in common with the super-mechanized State of Zamyatin's anti-Utopia. That writer's leaning towards primitivism was in line with a Russian tradition, with Slavophilism and hostility towards the bourgeois West, with the glorification of the *muzhik* and of the old patriarchal Russia, with Tolstoy and Dostoyevsky. Even as an émigré, Zamyatin was disillusioned with the West in the characteristically Russian fashion. At times he seemed half-reconciled with the Soviet régime when it was already producing its Benefactor in the person of Stalin. In so far as he directed the darts of his satire against Bolshevism, he did so on the ground that Bolshevism was bent on replacing the old primitive Russia by the modern, mechanized society. Curiously enough, he set his story in the year 2600; and he seemed to say to the Bolsheviks: this is what Russia will look like if you succeed in giving to your régime the background of Western technology. In Zamyatin, as in some other Russian intellectuals disillusioned with socialism, the hankering after the primitive modes of thought and life was natural in so far as primitivism was still strongly alive in the Russian background.

In Orwell there was and there could be no such authentic nostalgia after the pre-industrial society. Primitivism had no part in his experience and background, except during his stay in Burma, when he was hardly attracted by it. But he was terrified of the uses to which technology might be put by men determined to enslave society; and so he, too, came to question and satirize 'the implied aims of industrial civilization'.

Although his satire is more recognizably aimed at Soviet Russia than Zamyatin's, Orwell saw elements of Oceania in the England of his own days as well, not to speak of the United States. Indeed, the society of *1984* embodies all that he hated and disliked in his own surroundings: the drabness and monotony of the English industrial suburb, the 'filthy and grimy and smelly' ugliness of which he tried to match in his naturalistic, repetitive, and oppressive style; the food rationing and the government controls which he knew in war-time Britain; the 'rubbishy newspapers containing almost nothing except sport, crime, and astrology, sensational five-cent novelettes, films oozing with sex'; and so on. Orwell knew well that newspapers of this sort did not exist in Stalinist Russia, and that the faults of the Stalinist Press were of an altogether different kind. 'Newspeak' is much less a satire on the Stalinist idiom than on Anglo-American journalistic 'cablese', which he loathed and with which, as a working journalist, he was well familiar.

It is easy to tell which features of the party of *1984* satirize the British Labour Party rather than the Soviet Communist Party. Big Brother and his followers make no attempt to indoctrinate the working class, an omission Orwell would have been the last to ascribe to Stalinism. His Proles 'vegetate': 'heavy work, petty quarrels, films, gambling . . . fill their mental horizon.' Like the rubbishy newspapers and the films oozing with sex, so gambling, the new opium of the people, does not belong to the Russian scene. The Ministry of Truth is a transparent caricature of London's war-time Ministry of Information. The monster of Orwell's vision is, like every nightmare, made up of all sorts of faces and features and shapes, familiar and unfamiliar. Orwell's talent and originality are evident in the domestic aspect of his satire. But in the vogue which *1984* has enjoyed that aspect has rarely been noticed.

1984 is a document of dark disillusionment not only with Stalinism but with every form and shade of socialism. It is a cry from the abyss of despair. What plunged Orwell into that abyss? It was without any doubt the spectacle of the Stalinist Great Purges of 1936–8, the repercussions of which he experienced in Catalonia. As a man of sensitivity and integrity, he could not react to the purges otherwise than with anger and horror. His conscience could not be soothed by the Stalinist justifications and sophisms which at the time did soothe the conscience of, for instance, Arthur Koestler, a writer of greater brilliance and sophistication but of less moral resolution. The Stalinist justifications and sophisms were both *beneath* and *above* Orwell's level of reasoning —they were beneath and above the common sense and the stubborn empiricism of Billy Brown of London town, with whom Orwell identified himself even in his most rebellious or revolutionary moments. He was outraged, shocked, and shaken in his beliefs. He had never been a member of the Communist Party. But, as an adherent of the semi-Trotskyist P.O.U.M., he had, despite all his reservations, tacitly assumed a certain community of purpose and solidarity with the Soviet régime through all its vicissitudes and transformations, which were to him somewhat obscure and exotic.

The purges and their Spanish repercussions not only destroyed that community of purpose. Not only did he see the gulf between Stalinists and anti-Stalinists opening suddenly inside embattled Republican Spain. This, the immediate effect of the purges, was overshadowed by 'the irrational side of totalitarianism—human sacrifice, cruelty as an end in itself, the worship of a Leader', and 'the colour of the sinister slave-civilizations of the ancient world' spreading over contemporary society.

Like most British socialists, Orwell had never been a

Marxist. The dialectical-materialist philosophy had always been too abstruse for him. From instinct rather than consciousness he had been a staunch rationalist. The distinction between the Marxist and the rationalist is of some importance. Contrary to an opinion widespread in Anglo-Saxon countries, Marxism is not at all rationalist in its philosophy: it does not assume that human beings are, as a rule, guided by rational motives and that they can be argued into socialism by reason. Marx himself begins *Das Kapital* with the elaborate philosophical and historical inquiry into the 'fetishistic' modes of thought and behaviour rooted in 'commodity production'—that is, in man's work for, and dependence on, a market. The class struggle, as Marx describes it, is anything but a rational process. This does not prevent the rationalists of socialism describing themselves sometimes as Marxists. But the authentic Marxist may claim to be mentally better prepared than the rationalist is for the manifestations of irrationality in human affairs, even for such manifestations as Stalin's Great Purges. He may feel upset or mortified by them, but he need not feel shaken in his *Weltanschauung*, while the rationalist is lost and helpless when the irrationality of the human existence suddenly stares him in the face. If he clings to his rationalism, reality eludes him. If he pursues reality and tries to grasp it, he must part with his rationalism.

Orwell pursued reality and found himself bereft of his conscious and unconscious assumptions about life. In his thoughts he could not henceforth get away from the Purges. Directly and indirectly, they supplied the subject matter for nearly all that he wrote after his Spanish experience. This was an honourable obsession, the obsession of a mind not inclined to cheat itself comfortably and to stop grappling with an alarming moral problem. But grappling with the Purges, his mind became infected by their irrationality. He found himself incapable of explaining what was happening in terms which were familiar to him, the terms of empirical common sense. Abandoning rationalism, he increasingly viewed reality through the dark glasses of a quasi-mystical pessimism.

It has been said that *1984* is the figment of the imagination of a dying man. There is some truth in this, but not the whole truth. It was indeed with the last feverish flicker of life in him that Orwell wrote this book. Hence the extraordinary, gloomy intensity of his vision and language, and the almost physical immediacy with which he suffered the tortures which his creative imagination was inflicting on his chief character. He identified his own withering physical existence with the decayed and shrunken body of Winston Smith, to whom he imparted and in whom he invested, as it were, his own dying pangs. He projected the last spasms of his own suffering into the last pages of his last book. But the main explanation of the inner logic of Orwell's disillusionment and pessimism lies not in the writer's death agonies, but in the experience and the thought of the living man and in his convulsive reaction from his defeated rationalism.

'I understand HOW: I do not understand WHY' is the refrain of *1984*. Winston Smith knows how Oceania functions and how its elaborate mechanism of tyranny works, but he does not know what is its ultimate cause and ultimate purpose. He turns for the answer to the pages of '*the* book', the mysterious classic of 'crimethink', the authorship of which is attributed to Emmanuel Goldstein, the inspirer of the conspiratorial Brotherhood. But he manages to read through only those chapters of '*the* book' which deal with the HOW. The Thought Police descends upon him just when he is about to begin reading the chapters which promise to explain WHY; and so the question remains unanswered.

This was Orwell's own predicament. He asked the Why not so much about the Oceania of his vision as about Stalinism and the Great Purges. At one point he certainly turned for the answer to Trotsky: it was from Trotsky-Bronstein that he took the few sketchy biographical data and even the physiognomy and the Jewish name for Emmanuel Goldstein; and the fragments of '*the* book', which take up so many pages in *1984*, are an obvious, though not very successful, paraphrase of Trotsky's *The Revolution Betrayed*. Orwell was impressed by Trotsky's moral grandeur and at the same time he partly distrusted it and partly doubted its authenticity. The ambivalence of his view of Trotsky finds its counterpart in Winston Smith's attitude towards Goldstein. To the end Smith cannot find out whether Goldstein and the Brotherhood have ever existed in reality, and whether '*the* book' was not concocted by the Thought Police. The barrier between Trotsky's thought and himself, a barrier which Orwell could never break down, was Marxism and dialectical materialism. He found in Trotsky the answer to How, not to Why.

But Orwell could not content himself with historical agnosticism. He was anything but a sceptic. His mental make-up was rather that of the fanatic, determined to get an answer, a quick and a plain answer, to his question. He was now tense with distrust and suspicion and on the look-out for the dark conspiracies hatched by *them* against the decencies of Billy Brown of London town. *They* were the Nazis, the Stalinists, and—Churchill and Roosevelt, and ultimately all who had any *raison d'état* to defend, for at heart Orwell was a simple-minded anarchist and, in his eyes, any political movement forfeited its *raison d'être* the moment it acquired a *raison d'état*. To analyse a complicated social background, to try and unravel tangles of political motives, calculations, fears and suspicions, and to discern the compulsion of circumstances behind *their* action was beyond him. Generalizations about social forces, social trends, and historic inevitabilities made him bristle with suspicion. Yet, without some such generalizations, properly and sparingly used, no realistic answer could be given to the question which preoccupied Orwell. His gaze was fixed on the trees, or rather on a single tree, in front of him, and he was almost blind to the wood. Yet his distrust of historical generalizations led him in the end to adopt and to cling to the oldest, the most banal, the most abstract, the most metaphysical, and the most barren of all generalizations: all *their* conspiracies and plots and purges and diplomatic deals had one source and one source only—'sadistic power-hunger'. Thus he made his jump from workaday, rationalistic common sense to the mysticism of cruelty which inspires *1984*.[1]

In *1984* man's mastery over the machine has reached so high a level that society is in a position to produce plenty for everybody and put an end to inequality. But poverty and inequality are maintained only to satisfy the sadistic urges of Big Brother. Yet we do not even know whether Big Brother really exists—he may be only a myth. It is the collective cruelty of the party (not

[1] This opinion is based on personal reminiscences as well as on an analysis of Orwell's work. During the last war Orwell seemed attracted by the critical, then somewhat unusual, tenor of my commentaries on Russia which appeared in *The Economist*, *The Observer*, and *Tribune*. (Later we were both *The Observer*'s correspondents in Germany and occasionally shared a room in a Press camp.) However, it took me little time to become aware of the differences of approach behind our seeming agreement. I remember that I was taken aback by the stubbornness with which Orwell dwelt on 'conspiracies', and that his political reasoning struck me as a Freudian sublimation of persecution mania. He was, for instance, unshakably convinced that Stalin, Churchill, and Roosevelt consciously plotted to divide the world, and to divide it for good, among themselves, and to subjugate it in common. (I can trace the idea of Oceania, Eastasia, and Eurasia back to that time.) '*They* are all power-hungry,' he used to repeat. When once I pointed out to him that underneath the apparent solidarity of the Big Three one could discern clearly the conflict between them, already coming to the surface, Orwell was so startled and incredulous that he at once related our conversation in his column in *Tribune*, and added that he saw no sign of the approach of the conflict of which I spoke. This was by the time of the Yalta conference, or shortly thereafter, when not much foresight was needed to see what was coming. What struck me in Orwell was his lack of historical sense and of psychological insight into political life coupled with an acute, though narrow, penetration into some aspects of politics and with an incorruptible firmness of conviction.

necessarily of its individual members who may be intelligent and well-meaning people), that torments Oceania. Totalitarian society is ruled by a disembodied sadism. Orwell imagined that he had 'transcended' the familiar and, as he thought, increasingly irrelevant concepts of social class and class interest. But in these Marxist generalizations, the interest of a social class bears at least some specific relation to the individual interests and the social position of its members, even if the class interest does not represent a simple sum of the individual interests. In Orwell's party the whole bears no relation to the parts. The party is not a social body actuated by any interest or purpose. It is a phantom-like emanation of all that is foul in human nature. It is the metaphysical, mad and triumphant, Ghost of Evil.

Of course, Orwell intended 1984 as a warning. But the warning defeats itself because of its underlying boundless despair. Orwell saw totalitarianism as bringing history to a standstill. Big Brother is invincible: 'If you want a picture of the future, imagine a boot stamping on a human face—for ever.' He projected the spectacle of the Great Purges on to the future, and he saw it fixed there for ever, because he was not capable of grasping the events realistically, in their complex historical context. To be sure, the events were highly 'irrational'; but he who because of this treats them irrationally is very much like the psychiatrist whose mind becomes unhinged by dwelling too closely with insanity. 1984 is in effect not so much a warning as a piercing shriek announcing the advent of the Black Millennium, the Millennium of damnation.

The shriek, amplified by all the 'mass-media' of our time, has frightened millions of people. But it has not helped them to see more clearly the issues with which the world is grappling; it has not advanced their understanding. It has only increased and intensified the waves of panic and hate that run through the world and obfuscate innocent minds. 1984 has taught millions to look at the conflict between East and West in terms of black and white, and it has shown them a monster bogy and a monster scapegoat for all the ills that plague mankind.

At the onset of the atomic age, the world is living in a mood of Apocalyptic horror. That is why millions of people respond so passionately to the Apocalyptic vision of a novelist. The Apocalyptic atomic and hydrogen monsters, however, have not been let loose by Big Brother. The chief predicament of contemporary society is that it has not yet succeeded in adjusting its way of life and its social and political institutions to the prodigious advance of its technological knowledge. We do not know what has been the impact of the atomic and hydrogen bombs on the thoughts of millions in the East, where anguish and fear may be hidden behind the façade of a facile (or perhaps embarrassed?) official optimism. But it would be dangerous to blind ourselves to the fact that in the West millions of people may be inclined, in their anguish and fear, to flee from their own responsibility for mankind's destiny and to vent their anger and despair on the giant Bogy-cum-Scapegoat which Orwell's *1984* has done so much to place before their eyes.

* * *

'Have you read this book? You must read it, sir. Then you will know why we must drop the atom bomb on the Bolshies!' With these words a blind, miserable newsvendor recommended to me *1984* in New York, a few weeks before Orwell's death.

Poor Orwell, could he ever imagine that his own book would become so prominent an item in the programme of Hateweek?

PART TWO

HISTORICAL ESSAYS

TWO REVOLUTIONS[1]

AN eminent French historian once wrote: 'Consider the revolutions of the Renaissance: in them you will find all the passions, all the spirit, and all the language of the French revolution.' With some reservations, one might also say that if one considers the Great French revolution, one can find in it the passions, the spirit, and the language of the Russian revolution. This is true to such an extent that it is absolutely necessary for the student of recent Russian history to view it every now and then through the French prism. (The student of the French revolution, too, may gain new insights if occasionally he analyses his subject in the light of the Russian experience.) Historical analogy by itself is, of course, only one of the many angles from which he ought to approach his subject; and it may be downright misleading if he merely contents himself with assembling the points of formal resemblance between historical situations. 'History is concrete'; and this means, among other things, that every event or situation is unique, regardless of its possible similarity to other events and situations. In drawing any analogy, it is therefore important to know where the analogy ends. I hope that I shall not offend badly against this rule; and I would like to

[1] The publication of a French edition of *Stalin: A Political Biography* (English ed., New York and London, Oxford University Press, 1949) has given me an opportunity to comment on one aspect of that book, the analogies between the Russian and the French revolutions. These comments, written in 1950, appear here in substantially the same form as in the introduction to the French edition of *Stalin* (Paris, Gallimard).

acknowledge my great debt to the eminent French historians whose works on the French revolution have
helped me to gain new insights into the Russian revolution.

It is well known that the controversy over the 'Russian Thermidor' played in its time a great role in the
struggles inside the Bolshevik Party. Trotsky placed his
thesis about the Russian Thermidor in the very centre of
his denunciation of the Stalinist régime. This issue was
dealt with only indirectly in my political biography of
Stalin. (In my view, the Russian counterparts to the
Jacobin, Thermidorian, and Bonapartist phases of the
revolution have in a curious way overlapped and merged
in Stalinism.) A critical examination of this whole problem will be found in my forthcoming *Life of Trotsky*,
where it properly belongs. For the present I will concen-
trate on another perspective on recent Russian history,
a perspective somewhat similar to that which was drawn
by Albert Sorel in relation to the French revolution in
his monumental *L'Europe et la Révolution Française*. I
have in mind the reassertion of national tradition in a
revolutionary society.

The Bolshevik revolution of 1917 was in intention a
radical break with Russia's past, a break with her old
social outlook, with her old methods of government,
with her customs, habits, and traditions. It was a great
and stormy funeral of all the anachronisms inherited
from centuries of backwardness, serfdom, and tyranny.
The three post-revolutionary decades, however, saw a
complex and contradictory development: on the one
hand, Russia's advance, with gigantic strides, in industrialization and education, and a release of national
energies such as only a great revolution can produce; on
the other hand, an amazing resurrection of Russia's
buried past, and the revenge of that past upon the
present. It is as the embodiment of this contradictory
development that I wish to consider Stalin. To an almost
equal degree, Stalin represents the impetus given to

Russia by the revolution and the triumph of the traditions of the *ancien régime* over the original spirit of the
revolution. Yet, did not Napoleon I represent a similar
phenomenon? Were not the revolutionary and the *Roi
Soleil* blended in his personality as much as the Leninist
and Ivan the Terrible (or Peter the Great) are blended in
Stalin?

Those who are interested mainly in the individual
psychology of historical personalities may be outraged
by this comparison. Stalin, they may object, has none of
the *élan*, the *esprit*, the charm, and nothing of the originality of mind and expression with which nature so richly
endowed Bonaparte. This is willingly admitted. But we
are concerned here with something else, with the respective functions of the two personalities in the history of
their countries; and these ought to be viewed in the light
of broader, impersonal factors, of the moving forces, the
motives and objectives of the two revolutions, and in the
light of their different social backgrounds and national
traditions. Incidentally, even the contrast between the
individual characteristics of the two men fits in with and
can up to a point be explained by the contrast between
their national backgrounds and traditions. Napoleon, the
Emperor, descended indirectly from an absolute monarchy, the chief representative of which appears, in historical idealization, as the *Roi Soleil*. The Tsar who in a
sense is Stalin's political ancestor could earn, even from
his apologists, no brighter epithet than *Grozny*—the
Awe-inspiring. Napoleon has the clear air, bright colour,
and elegance of Versailles and Fontainebleau as his
background; while Stalin's figure harmonizes with the
grim *ambiance* of the Kremlin. Thus, even the individual
temper of the two men seems to reflect something
impersonal.

Albert Sorel describes how heavily tradition weighed
upon the revolution: 'Events hurled them [the members
of the Convention] abruptly into power: if they had had
a taste for liberty, they would have had no spare time to

serve an apprenticeship in it.'[1] The leaders of the Russian Soviets had just as little spare time in which to serve an apprenticeship in liberty as had the leaders of the Convention. 'At the beginning of the revolution, the minds of men rushed towards the ideal: everything was destroyed, everything was renewed; France was re-created, so to speak, after having been annihilated. . . . Disorder, anarchy, civil war ensued. Foreign war was added. The revolution was threatened, France invaded. The Republicans had to defend at one and the same time the independence of the nation, the territory of the homeland, the principles of the Revolution, the supremacy of their party, even their own lives. . . . With pure reason confounded, they fell back brutally on empiricism: they turned from instinct to custom, to routine, to precedents: none were for liberty, countless numbers were for despotism. Thus all the processes of government of the *ancien régime* were seen to insinuate themselves, in the name of expedience, into the revolution. Once having regained their place, they remained there as masters. All the theoreticians' art consisted of nothing more than masking and disguising them.'[2] How admirably these words suit the fortunes of the Russian revolution as well!

Yet, while it is right to point to this reassertion of tradition, a reassertion that some may regard as natural and sound and others may view as a distortion of the revolution, it would be wrong to see in the post-revolutionary régime nothing but a prolongation of the *ancien régime*. Under the Empire, French history did not merely pick up the threads that had been violently snapped by the Convention; it wove the pattern of a new France and it worked the threads of tradition into that new pattern. The same may be said of Stalinist Russia. She may feel the revenge of the past on herself, but she does not

[1] Albert Sorel, *L'Europe et la Révolution Française* (third ed., Paris, 1893), Part 1, p. 224.

[2] Albert Sorel, *L'Europe et la Révolution Française*, pp. 224–5.

revert to that past. The Bourbon monarchy could never have produced anything like the Napoleonic Code, that legal-philosophical mirror of a bourgeois society. Similarly, planned economy could never have come into existence within the framework of the old Russia. To make it possible, nothing less than the October Revolution was needed; and in it, in the principle and the practice of the planned economy, the October Revolution has survived and developed, despite the insinuation of 'all the processes of government of the *ancien régime*'.

In the case of the Russian revolution, it would be even more unrealistic than in that of the French to deny or overlook what is essentially new and epoch-making in its achievement. There may have been some justification for Sorel's view that if the French revolution had not taken place, the *ancien régime* would, in the course of time, have done some of the work that was accomplished only after its overthrow.[1] The point is that within the shell of France's *ancien régime* the elements of a modern bourgeois society had achieved a relatively high degree of maturity; the revolution merely broke the shell and thereby facilitated and speeded up the organic growth and development of those elements. Even so, historians like Michelet, Jaurès, and others, who stressed the essentially new and creative work of the revolution, seem nearer the truth than Sorel, whose emphasis on historical continuity, so original and illuminating in many respects, appears in others to be exaggerated and essentially conservative. In the case of Russia, the limits within which the law of historical continuity operates are undoubtedly much narrower. The elements of the present collectivist society, with its planned economy—let us leave aside whether this society deserves to be called socialist or not —hardly existed under the surface of Russia's *ancien régime*. They are largely the conscious creation of the revolution and of the post-revolutionary government. As

[1] This idea was, of course, developed before Sorel by Alexis de Tocqueville in *L'Ancien Régime*.

a builder of a new economy and a pioneer of new social techniques, Stalin, for all his limitations and vices—the limitations of an empiricist and the vices of a despot—is likely to leave deeper marks on history than any single French revolutionary leader. Here perhaps is the point at which the difference in the very nature of the two revolutions tends to make further comparisons misleading.

Let us now try to investigate how far the analogy holds good in a different field—in the French revolution's foreign policy, in its impact on the world and the world's impact on it. Sorel, who surveyed this vast field with the greatest thoroughness and understanding, tells us that 'To come to terms with the French revolution, the old Europe abdicated its principles; to come to terms with the old Europe, the French revolution falsified its own. France had solemnly renounced conquests. . . . Victory made the revolution bellicose. The war, begun for the defence of French territory, continued for the invasion of neighbouring territories. After having conquered in order to liberate, France partitioned in order to retain.'[1] Reading this, one cannot help thinking of Yalta and Potsdam, where by acquiescing in the expansion of Stalinist Russia the statesmen of the capitalist West so clearly abdicated their principles, while Stalinist Russia, by insisting on strategic frontiers and on the absorption of most of the neighbouring lands which had once been conquered by the Tsars, so flagrantly falsified her own. Is it really true that history does not repeat itself? Or that in the repetition the original drama becomes a farce? Is it not rather that in its Russian repetition the French tragedy appears magnified and intensified, projected as it is from the European to the global scale and from an epoch preceding the steam engine to the age of atomic energy?

Let us once again compare the original with the repetition: 'Not being able to destroy all the monarchies, she [the revolution] was forced to come to terms with the

[1] Albert Sorel, *L'Europe et la Révolution Française*, p. 3.

monarchs. She vanquished her enemies, she pursued them on their own territory, she effected magnificent conquests; but to keep them at peace, it was necessary to treat; to treat, it was necessary to negotiate, and to negotiate was to return to custom. The *ancien régime* and the revolution compromised not on principles which were irreconcilable, but on frontiers which were changeable. There existed only one idea in common on which the old Europe and Republican France could understand each other and come to an agreement: it was *raison d'état*. It ruled their treaties. The territories not having changed their places, and the ambitions of States remaining what they were, all the traditions of the old statecraft were reborn in the negotiations. These traditions accorded only too well with the designs of the revolutionaries . . . they placed at the service of the victorious revolution the methods of the *ancien régime*.'[1] While from the angle of the internal development of the revolution it may be said that up to a point the phases corresponding to Jacobinism, Thermidorianism, and Bonapartism have merged in Stalinism, in its foreign policy during the Second World War victorious Stalinism simply put to its service the methods of the *ancien régime*. I have described in my book how at Potsdam and Yalta Stalin's 'conduct, aspirations, methods of action, even his gestures and caprices vividly resembled the behaviour, the aspirations, and gestures of Tsar Alexander I at the conclusion of the Napoleonic wars.'[2] And what was Stalin's conception of the preponderance of the Great Powers and of the division between them of spheres of influence if not that old *raison d'état*, the only idea which he held in common with Churchill and Roosevelt? That this *raison d'état* agreed, in a way, with a revolutionary design subsequent events were to reveal.

Russia, like France before her, has carried her revolution abroad. It was not, let us note, in the Jacobin and

[1] Albert Sorel, *L'Europe et la Révolution Française*, pp. 544–5.
[2] *Stalin*, p. 530.

Republican period that Europe caught the revolutionary infection from France. And it was not in the heroic, Leninist period that the Bolshevik revolution spread beyond Russian frontiers. The two revolutions were carried abroad by rulers who had first tamed those revolutions at home. 'The revolution was arrested in France and in a way congealed in military despotism; but, by the very action of that despotism, it continued to propagate itself in Europe. Conquest spread it among the peoples. Although greatly degenerated, it retained enough appeal to excite them. . . .'[1] And again: 'It was in that form that the revolution appeared to have arrested itself and fixed itself in France; it was in that form that Europe understood it and imitated it.'[2] It is in its Stalinist, and not in its Leninist and Trotskyist form that the revolution has come to a halt and has fixed itself in Russia, and it is in this form that it has spread, to the amazement of disillusioned ex-communists who have difficulty understanding how a revolution so 'greatly degenerated' has been able to retain so much appeal.[3]

Like Bonapartist France, Stalinist Russia has created a whole system of satellites. In this Stalin might find a grave warning to himself. It was the revolt of its own satellites that contributed so signally to the downfall of the Bonapartist empire. Two of these satellites, Prussia and Italy, inflicted on France some of its most severe setbacks. It was an Italian patriot who wrote in 1814 the following significant words: 'It is painful for me to say it, for no one feels more than I the gratitude which we owe Napoleon; no one appreciates better than I the value of each drop of that generous French blood which watered the Italian soil and redeemed it; but I must be permitted to say it, for it is the truth: to see the French depart was an immense, an ineffable joy.' We have heard

[1] Albert Sorel, *L'Europe et la Révolution Française*, pp. 4–5.
[2] Albert Sorel, *L'Europe et la Révolution Française*, p. 548.
[3] The reader will find a more detailed discussion of this point in *Stalin*, Chapters XIII and XIV.

Tito uttering similar words about the Russians, and who knows how many Eastern European communists would be happy to utter them if they could? To Bonaparte, and many of his compatriots, the behaviour of Italy and Prussia looked like the height of ingratitude. So does the behaviour of Tito to Stalin. But what is it that gives rise to that 'ingratitude'?

Neither of these systems of satellites has lacked redeeming features. 'In the countries which France united with her territory or constituted in her image,' says Sorel, 'she proclaimed her principles, destroyed the feudal system, and introduced her laws. After the inevitable disorders of war and the first excesses of conquest, this revolution constituted an immense benefit to the peoples. This is why the conquests of the Republic could not be confused with the conquests of the *ancien régime*. They differed in the essential characteristic that, despite the abuse of principles and the deviations of ideas, the work of France was accomplished for the nations.'[1] Without repeating here my analysis of our contemporary counterpart to this phenomenon, I shall only say that I do not believe that the verdict of history on the Stalinist system of satellites will in this respect be more severe than it has been on the Bonapartist system.[2] However, the French system of satellites was not saved by its redeeming features. It would be difficult to find a more brilliant and more convincing explanation of this fact than the one offered by Sorel:

'The French republicans believed themselves to be cosmopolitans, but they were that only in their speeches; they felt, they thought, they acted, they interpreted their universal ideas and their abstract principles in accordance

[1] Albert Sorel, *L'Europe et la Révolution Française*, p. 547.

[2] I was brought up in Poland, one of Napoleon's satellite countries, where even in my day the Napoleonic legend was so strongly alive that, as a schoolboy, I wept bitter tears over Napoleon's downfall, as nearly every Polish child did. And now I live in England, where most schoolchildren, I am sure, still rejoice over the story of the defeat of Napoleon, that villain of the English traditionalist historians.

with the traditions of a conquering monarchy. . . .
They identified humanity with their homeland, their
national cause with the cause of all the nations. Consequently and entirely naturally, they confused the propagation of new doctrines with the extension of French
power, the emancipation of humanity with the grandeur
of the Republic, the reign of reason with that of France,
the liberation of peoples with the conquest of States, the
European revolution with the domination of the French
revolution in Europe . . . they established subservient
and subordinate republics which they held in a sort of
tutelage. . . . The revolution degenerated into an armed
propaganda, then into conquest. . . .'[1] In the same way,
the Russian Stalinists think of themselves as interna-
tionalists, but they feel, think, and act with the tradition
of a conquering monarchy behind them; and so they,
too, confuse the emancipation of mankind with the
grandeur of their republic and the reign of reason with
the rule of Russia. No wonder that the reaction of the
satellite peoples tends to take a familiar form: 'The
peoples easily understood this language [of emancipation spoken by the revolution]. . . . What they did not
understand at all was that, using this language, . . . she
[France] aimed at enslaving them and exploited them.
They made no distinction, moreover, between her and
the man who governed her; they did not investigate the
phases through which the French revolution had passed,
and how the Republic had transformed itself into an
empire; they knew the revolution only in the form of
conquest . . . and it was in that form that, even by virtue
of its principles, they came to abhor it. They rose against
its domination.'[2] We are not prophesying here a rising
of the peoples against Stalinist domination. But there
can be little doubt that the peoples of Eastern and Central Europe, who might have understood well the language of social emancipation spoken by Russia, cannot

[1] Albert Sorel, *L'Europe et la Révolution Française*, pp. 541–2.
[2] Albert Sorel, *L'Europe et la Révolution Française*, p. 5.

understand why they should become subordinate to Russia; that they, and others, make no distinction now between the Russian revolution and 'the man who governs her'; that they are not interested in the stages by which the Republic of the Workers' and Peasants' Councils has become transformed into something like an empire; and that they know the Russian revolution largely in the form of conquest.

Having indulged in these comparisons, I cannot but point out where and why this broad historical analogy ceases to apply. I shall not dwell on the obvious differences—in some respects important, in others irrelevant —between two revolutions, one of which was bourgeois in character and the other proletarian, at least in origin. Nor shall I expatiate on the major differences between the international scene as it looks now and as it looked a century and a half ago. But a few words ought perhaps to be said on one important development—the Chinese revolution—which has come to light only very recently.

The lightning collapse of the Kuomintang and the absolute victory of the communist armies have clearly altered the international balance of power. In the long run, the Chinese revolution must also have its repercussions inside Russia. This revolution obviously deserves to be placed in a different category from the 'revolutions from above' that took place in Eastern and Central Europe in the years 1945–8. The latter were mainly the by-products of Russia's military victory: 'Although the local Communist Parties were its immediate agents and executors, the great party of the revolution, which remained in the background, was the Red Army.'[1] In contrast to this, even though it may have drawn moral inspiration from Russia, Chinese communism can rightly claim that its revolution has been its own work and its own achievement. The very magnitude of the Chinese revolution and its intrinsic momentum have been such

[1] *Stalin*, p. 554.

that it is ludicrous to consider it as anybody's puppet creation. This is not a satellite of the Russian revolution, but another great upheaval in its own right. For this phenomenon we find no parallel in the epoch of the French revolution. To its very end the French revolution stood alone. One can only think of an imaginary analogy: one may wonder what Europe would look like if, at the turn of the eighteenth and nineteenth centuries, Germany, then disunited and backward, had carried out more or less independently its own version of the French revolution. A combination of a Jacobin or Bonapartist France with a unified, Jacobin Germany might have given history a direction different from that which France alone could impart to it. Perhaps there would have been no Waterloo. Or perhaps the anti-revolutionary forces of Europe would have joined hands much earlier and more resolutely than they did against France alone.

Both Stalinists and anti-Stalinists have recently begun to foster the legend that Stalin has been the actual inspirer of the Chinese revolution. How is this to be reconciled with his role in the events in China in 1925-7? How is this to be squared with Stalin's own statement at Potsdam that 'the Kuomintang is the only political force capable of ruling China'?[1] It may be argued that at Potsdam he was ostensibly disavowing the Chinese communists only to trick his Western allies. But this was hardly the case. The version of events which seems much nearer to the truth is that until very late in the day Stalin had a low opinion of the ability of the Communist Party to bring China under its control, and that he went so far as to attempt, even in 1948, to dissuade Mao Tse-tung from launching the series of offensives which was to bring victory to Chinese communism. A letter from Stalin to Mao to this effect was apparently read at the Conference of the Chinese Communist Party that took

[1] For instance, see James F. Byrnes, *Speaking Frankly* (New York, 1947), p. 228.

place shortly before the opening of the offensive; but the Conference rejected Stalin's advice.[1]

In his untimely scepticism about the Chinese revolution, Stalin appears true to character. He made a similar miscalculation in the middle 1920's, before Chiang Kai-shek started his great march to the north. In March 1926, the Russian Politbureau discussed whether it should encourage Chiang (then still Moscow's ally and honorary member of the Executive of the Comintern) in his plans for the conquest of the whole of China. Stalin insisted that Chiang be advised to content himself with the area in the south, where he was in actual control, and to seek a *modus vivendi* with Chang Tso-lin's government which still controlled the north. Chiang disregarded this advice and shortly thereafter established his control over all of China. More than two decades later, Stalin again seems to have overrated the stability of an old and decaying régime and underrated the revolutionary forces opposed to it. With much more justification than Tito, Mao Tse-tung might therefore say that not only was his régime not created by force of Russian arms, but that he secured its triumph against Moscow's explicit advice.

Whatever the truth about Stalin's role in these events, the Chinese revolution is likely to affect strongly the fortunes of Stalinism. In my book, Stalinism was shown to be primarily the product of the isolation of Russian

[1] In *The Times*, a Special Correspondent wrote on his return from Peking: '. . . there is much evidence to suggest that the Kremlin did not anticipate the sweeping victory which Chinese Communism was so soon to gain. . . . As late as July 1948 the Russians neither expected nor desired an immediate Communist victory in China. In that month the Chinese Communist Party held a conference to discuss plans for the coming autumn campaign. The advice from Russia was to continue guerrilla warfare for the coming year in order to weaken America, who was expected to continue to pour arms into China in support of the Kuomintang. Russia opposed any plan to end the civil war by taking the large cities. Russian advice was rejected by this conference, the contrary policy was adopted. . . .' *The Times*, 27 June 1950. Similar reports have appeared in many other papers.

Bolshevism in a capitalist world and of the mutual assimilation of the isolated revolution with the Russian
tradition. The victory of Chinese communism marks the
end of that isolation; and it does so much more decisively
than did the spread of Stalinism in Eastern Europe. Thus,
one major precondition for the emergence of Stalinism
now belongs to the past. This should stimulate processes
inside Russia, tending to overcome that strange ideology
and frame of mind which formed themselves in the
period of isolation. Yet we know how often in history
effects do outlast causes; and for how long they do so!

While in one of its repercussions the Chinese revolution tends to deprive Stalinism of its *raison d'être*, in
another it tends to strengthen and consolidate it. Stalinism has not only been the product of isolated Bolshevism; it has also reflected the ascendancy of the Oriental,
semi-Asiatic and Asiatic, over the European element in
Russia, and consequently in the revolution. Mao Tse-
tung's victory enhances that element and imparts to it
immense additional weight. How much more real must
his own *Ex Oriente Lux* sound to Stalin himself now than
it did in 1918, when he published it! So much indeed
has the Oriental element come to predominate in the
whole international communist movement that the
struggle between communism and anti-communism is
more and more becoming identified, not only geographi-
cally, with the antagonism between East and West. The
fact that communism is in its origin a Western idea *par
excellence* and that the West exported it to Russia is
almost forgotten. Having conquered the East and absorbed its climate and traditions, communism in its
Stalinist form not only fails to understand the West, but
itself becomes more and more incomprehensible to the
West. In Russia, the Greek Orthodox and Byzantine
tradition has refracted itself in the revolution. Will the
Confucian tradition now similarly refract itself through
Chinese communism?

The political history of Stalin is a tale not lacking in

grimness and cruelty, but one ought perhaps to be cautioned against drawing from it a moral of disillusionment or despair, for the story is not yet finished. Nearly every great revolution has destroyed as many hopes as it has fulfilled; every revolution therefore has left behind it an aftermath of frustration and cynicism. As a rule, men have been able to do full justice to the whole experience only from a long perspective of time. 'What do we know, after all?' Louis Blanc once wrote in a similar context. 'In order that progress be realized, perhaps it is necessary that all evil alternatives be exhausted. The life of mankind is very long, and the number of possible solutions very limited. All revolution is useful, in this sense at least, that every revolution takes care of one dangerous alternative. Because from an unfortunate state of affairs societies sometimes tumble into a worse state, let us not hasten to conclude that progress is a chimera.'[1] Let us not hasten to do so.

[1] Louis Blanc, *Histoire de Dix Ans* (10th ed., Paris, n.d.), I, 135.

MARX AND RUSSIA[1]

THE attitudes of Marx and Engels towards Russia and their views on the prospects of Russian revolution form a curious topic in the history of socialism. Did the founders of scientific socialism have any premonition of the great upheaval in Russia that was to be carried out under the sign of Marxism? What results did they expect from the social developments inside the Tsarist Empire? How did they view the relationship between revolutionary Russia and the West? One can answer these questions more fully now on the basis of the correspondence between Marx, Engels, and their Russian contemporaries, published by the Marx-Engels-Lenin Institute in Moscow last year. This correspondence covers nearly half a century. It opens with Marx's well-known letters to Anenkov of 1846. It closes with the correspondence between Engels and his Russian friends in 1895. The volume also contains nearly fifty letters published for the first time.

Among the Russians who kept in touch with Marx and Engels there were men and women belonging to three generations of revolutionaries. In the 'forties the revolutionary movement in Russia had an almost exclusively intellectual and liberal character. It was based on no social class or popular force. To that epoch belonged Marx's early correspondents, Anenkov, Sazonov, and a few others. Marx explained to them his philosophy and his economic ideas, but engaged in no discussion on revolution in Russia. For this it was too early. Broadly speaking, in those years Russia was to Marx still identical with

[1] B.B.C. Third Programme talk, November 1948.

Tsardom, and Tsardom was the hated 'gendarme of European reaction'. His and Engels' main preoccupation was to arouse Europe against that gendarme, for they believed that a European war against Russia would hasten the progress of the West towards socialism.

In the 'sixties another generation of Russian revolutionaries came to the fore. They were the Narodniks or Populists or Agrarian socialists. It was, curiously enough, with the Russian intellectuals of that school advocating a pure peasant socialism that the two founders of the Western, strictly proletarian, socialism established ties of the closest friendship. Russia possessed no industry yet, no modern working class, almost no bourgeoisie. The intelligentsia and the peasantry were the only forces inside Russia to whom the two sworn enemies of Tsardom could look. There was, of course, also Bakunin's anarchism. Marx first co-operated with Bakunin and then quarrelled with him. But I shall not discuss that controversy, to which only casual references occur in the correspondence under review. Incidentally, *vis-à-vis* Marx, Bakunin acted more as the spokesman of Italian, Swiss, and Spanish anarchists than as a Russian revolutionary.

The Narodniks in Russia and in exile eagerly responded to the theories of Marx and Engels. Russian was the first language into which *Das Kapital* was translated from the original. Based on English classical economy and German philosophy and on a thorough study of Western industrial capitalism, this great work seemed to bear no direct relation to the social conditions then prevailing in Russia. And yet right from the beginning when it was making no impression on the Western European public, Marx's *opus* exercised an enormous influence upon the Russian intelligentsia. Danielson, the translator of *Das Kapital*, himself a prominent Narodnik and economist, wrote to Marx that the Russian censor passed the book, believing it to be too strictly scientific to be suppressed. The book, so the censor thought, made in any case too heavy reading to have any subversive influence. He was more afraid of the frontispiece of the Russian edition with Marx's portrait, and, allowing Marx's ideas to reach the Russian public, he confiscated his picture. Some years later the Russian censor passed the second volume of *Das Kapital* too, even though he had shortly before confiscated a Russian edition of the works of good old Adam Smith. Nine hundred copies of *Das Kapital* were sold out in St. Petersburg within a few weeks after its publication in 1872, a very large number considering the character of the book, the time, and the place. But even before that Marx received striking proof of strange Russian enthusiasm for his ideas, when on 12 March 1870 a group of Russian revolutionaries asked him to represent Russia on the General Council of the first International.

Marx was slightly puzzled by this unexpected Russian enthusiasm; 'A funny position for me', he wrote to Engels, 'to be functioning as the representative of young Russia! A man never knows what he may come to, or what strange fellowship he may have to submit to.' But ironical amusement was only one part, perhaps the least essential, of Marx's reaction to Russian admiration. His mind was agitated by Russia as a social phenomenon. At the age of fifty he and Engels began to learn Russian. They watched the development of Russian literature and swallowed volume after volume of Russian statistics and sociology. Marx even intended to re-write a portion of *Das Kapital* so as to base it on his Russian findings, an intention he was never able to carry out. Although amusement at some Russian eccentricities never left them, both Marx and Engels acquired a profound respect for the Russian intellectual achievement. Chernyshevsky, then serving his term of slave labour in Siberia, impressed Marx as the most original contemporary thinker and economist. He planned to arouse protests in Western Europe against the victimization of Chernyshevsky, but Chernyshevsky's friends feared that foreign protest and intervention might do more harm than good to the great convict. Dobrolyubov, who had died at the age of twenty-five, was another Russian thinker highly valued by Marx as 'a writer of the stature of a Lessing or a Diderot'. Finally, in 1884, Engels wrote to Madame Papritz, a Russian singer, and translator of Engels:

'We both, Marx and myself, cannot complain about your countrymen. If in some groups there was more revolutionary muddle than scientific research, there was also, on the other hand, critical thought and disinterested investigation in the field of pure theory, worthy of the nation of Dobrolyubov and Chernyshevsky . . . I have in mind not only the active revolutionary socialists, but also the historical and critical school in Russian literature, which is infinitely superior to anything achieved by respectable historians in Germany and France.'

But the main issue of the correspondence was Russia's road to socialism. In the West, capitalist industrialization was, according to Marx and Engels, paving the way for socialism. The industrial working class was the main force interested in socialism. But what about Russia, where capitalist industry had not even begun to strike roots? The Narodniks argued that Russian socialism would be based on the primeval rural commune or the *obshchina*, which had existed alongside of feudalism. Even after the emancipation of the serfs in 1861, the peasant land was still owned by the rural commune, in some respects the forerunner of the present Russian *kolkhoz*. Russia, said the Narodniks, need not go through the trials and tribulations of capitalist industrialism to attain socialism. She finds socialism in her native rural tradition, which she only needs to cleanse of feudal remnants. This then was to be Russia's road to socialism, very different from that by which Western Europe was expected to travel.

Most, though not all, Narodniks were Slavophils and believed in Russia's peculiar socialist mission. Marx, as we know, rejected Slavophilism; and nothing made him more furious than the talk about Russia's socialist mis-

sion. He did not believe, he once said, that old Europe
needed to be rejuvenated by Russian blood. But he did,
nevertheless, share some of the hopes that the Narodniks
placed on the Russian rural commune. Here, he said, in
a famous letter to a Russian periodical in 1877, here was
'the finest chance ever offered by history to any nation',
the chance to escape capitalism and to pass from feudalism straight into socialism. True, Marx added important qualifications: the rural commune had begun to
disintegrate, and if that process were to continue Russia
would miss her 'finest chance'. Moreover, a stimulus
from outside, the socialist transformation of Western
Europe, was needed to enable Russia to build socialism
on the rural commune. In his eyes Western Europe had
the birthright of socialist revolution, while Russia's role
could be secondary only. Nevertheless, Russia might
have her own short cut to socialism.

He and Engels also sympathized with the terrorism of
the Narodniks, with their attempts on the life of the Tsar
and his satraps. When, in 1881, revolutionaries assas-
sinated Tsar Alexander II, Marx and Engels applauded
the deed. In a message to a Russian meeting comme-
morating the tenth anniversary of the Paris commune,
they expressed the hope that the assassination of the
Tsar foreshadowed 'the formation of a Russian commune'. Here we reach the most dramatic point in the
whole correspondence. By the time of the assassination
of Alexander II a new generation of revolutionaries, the
first real Russian Marxists, had entered politics. Their
chief spokesmen were George Plekhanov, Vera Zasulich,
and Paul Axelrod, the future founders of Russian social
democracy. These first Russian Marxists were bitterly
opposed to the Narodniks precisely on those points in
which Marx and Engels had supported them. The young
Marxists opposed terrorism. Plekhanov in particular had
regarded the planned assassination of the Tsar as a sense-
less adventure. He believed that the task of Russian
revolutionaries was to abolish the autocratic system, not

to kill an autocrat. The Russian Marxists further believed that like Western Europe Russia had to go through capitalist industrialization and the experience of democratic self-government before she could even begin to evolve in the direction of socialism. They held that the rural commune was irretrievably disintegrating and was of no use to socialism. They placed their hopes not on the peasants but on the industrial working class now beginning to grow, not on agrarian but on proletarian socialism.

Both Narodniks and Marxists quoted *Das Kapital* as their authority. The Marxists had reason to expect that the two great Western socialists would agree with them that Russia was destined to go through the same evolution that Western Europe had gone through. One can therefore imagine their disappointment when Marx himself cold-shouldered them. In a letter to Vera Zasulich of 1881 Marx told them that it was no use to quote *Das Kapital* against the Narodniks and the rural commune, for in *Das Kapital* he had analysed the social structure of Western Europe only—Russia might well evolve towards socialism in her own way. Marx admitted that the rural commune had begun to decay, but on balance he still subscribed to the Narodnik view that the commune had a great future. Nor was Marx impressed by indignant arguments against Narodnik terrorism, although he regarded it as a 'specifically Russian and historically inevitable method about which there is no reason . . . to moralize for or against'. He would, of course, have none of that terrorism in Western Europe.

In 1883 Marx died and Engels took over the correspondence. The Russian Marxists tried to convert the surviving founding father of the Marxist school to their view. At first they were unsuccessful. Engels persisted in the hope that the Narodnik terrorist attempts would lead to the overthrow of Tsardom. In 1884 and 1885 he expected dramatic political changes inside Russia. Russia, he wrote, was approaching her 1789. Recalling the assassination of the Tsar four years after the event, he said that this was 'one of the exceptional cases in which a handful of men could make a revolution', a view that the young Russian Marxists, hoping for revolution by a social class and not by a 'handful of men', had already derided as a dangerous illusion. 'Every month now', Engels wrote to Vera Zasulich in 1884, 'ought to aggravate Russia's domestic difficulties. If some constitutionally minded and courageous Grand Duke were to appear now, even the Russian upper classes would find that a palace revolution was the best way out of the impasse.' One can imagine the ironical smile with which Plekhanov and Zasulich tried to disillusion him but in vain. We now know that in this controversy it was the Russian Marxists and not Marx and Engels whom events proved to be right. The assassination of Alexander II in fact entailed the disintegration and demoralization of the Narodnik movement and a prolonged period of reaction. This cool attitude of Marx and Engels towards their Russian followers was marked by intellectual inconsistency. But it was understandable and very human. The Narodniks had been Marx's close and admired friends, the first to raise the banner of popular revolution, the first to respond, in their own Slavonic manner, to Marxism. The Narodnik views had now become outdated. But an old loyalty and, no doubt, remoteness from the Russian scene prevented Marx and Engels from grasping this as quickly as their young Russian pupils had done it.

Only in the early 'nineties, towards the end of his life, Engels at last realized that Plekhanov and Zasulich had been right, that the rural commune was doomed, that capitalism was invading Russia and that the agrarian brand of socialism had to give way to the industrial one. He tried to impress his new view upon the old Narodniks, especially upon Danielson, the translator of *Das Kapital*. The letters that now passed between Danielson and Engels make melancholy reading. Danielson vented his disappointment with Engels' new attitude. He described very eloquently the evils of capitalism in Russia, suggesting that by its insistence on the need for Russia to go through the capitalist phase Marxism acted as *advocatus diaboli*. He reminded Engels what great store Marx had set by the Russian rural commune. In reply Engels argued seriously, patiently, and gently, very gently indeed, that new social processes had taken place, that in the meantime the rural commune had become part of a 'dead past', and that though the evils of capitalism were so great, Russia could unfortunately not escape them. 'History', said Engels, 'is the most cruel of all goddesses. She drives her triumphal chariot over heaps of corpses, not only during war, but even in times of "peaceful" economic development.'

This was a reference to the disastrous Russian drought and famine of 1891, which Danielson had blamed on incipient capitalist disorganization in agriculture. The rural commune, Engels went on, would have become the basis for Russian socialism, if in the industrial West socialism had won 'some ten or twenty years ago. Unfortunately, we [that is the West] have been too slow.' Which were the symptoms? The loss by England of her industrial monopoly, the industrial competition between France, Germany, and England. 'America', Engels wrote in 1893, 'bids fair to drive them all out of the world's markets. . . . The introduction of a, at least relative, free-trade policy in America is sure to complete the ruin of England's industrial position and to destroy, at the same time, the industrial export trade of Germany and France; then the crisis must come. . . .' Meanwhile capitalism still dominated the West, and Russia, too, must come within its orbit. This delay in the march of socialism was deplorable. But, said Engels, 'we . . . are unfortunately so stupid that we never can pluck up courage for a real progress unless urged to it by sufferings that seem almost out of proportion' to the goal to be achieved.

It is now easy to see that in this controversy both sides were right and wrong at the same time. Engels, converted to the view of his young Russian disciples, was of course right when he said that Russia could not avoid becoming capitalist. But the old Narodnik Danielson was also right in his insistence that Russian capitalism would have little scope for development because the terrifying poverty of the Russian peasants would limit to a minimum its home market and because Russia was too weak to compete with other nations in foreign markets. It was precisely this weakness in Russian capitalism, a weakness not clearly seen either by Engels or by the early Russian Marxists, that led in the last instance to the Bolshevik revolution of 1917. It was this weakness that was to make of Russia, in Lenin's words, the 'weakest link in the chain of capitalism'.

Nevertheless, Engels had a strong premonition of the coming Russian revolution. Repeatedly he stated that 'Russia was the France of the new age'. On his death-bed almost, in 1895, he watched the first moves of the new, and the last, Russian Tsar Nicolas II, and in a letter to Plekhanov he prophesied: 'If the devil of revolution has taken anybody by the scruff of the neck then it is Tsar Nicolas II.' But what Engels apparently expected to occur in Russia was 'another 1789', another anti-feudal, bourgeois revolution, not a socialist one.

Even towards the end of his life, after he had intellectually detached himself from the Narodniks, Engels still refused to criticize them in public. Plekhanov and Zasulich repeatedly urged him to do so and thus to further the cause of Russian Marxism. Engels then somewhat apologetically explained to Plekhanov his extremely delicate attitude towards the old Narodniks:

'It is quite impossible to argue with Russians of that generation . . . who still believe in the spontaneously communistic mission, which allegedly distinguishes Russia, the true holy Russia, from all other infidel countries. . . . Incidentally, in a country like yours . . . surrounded by a more or less solid intellectual Chinese Wall, erected by despotism, one should not be surprised by the appearance of the most incredible and queer combinations of ideas.'

With this note of an almost sorrowful understanding for the limitations of his old Narodnik friends, Engels' correspondence came to an end.

TROTSKY ON STALIN[1]

Trotsky's 'appraisal' of Stalin is one of the tragic documents in modern literature. The contemporary reader cannot yet look either at the hero of this book or at its author in the perspective of history, and hence it is not easy to define its value as a document. The train of events, to which the feud of the two men belongs, has not yet run its full course. Even the publication of the book has, regardless of its author's intentions, become a minor incident in the contemporary controversy between East and West. The book was ready for publication in the United States as early as 1941. It was then withheld from print by the American publishers, in deference to the leader of a mighty allied nation. It first saw the light (in the United States) only in 1946, after the Foreign Secretaries of the former allies had fallen out, and opinion had made the remarkable swing from wartime admiration of Russia to acute peacetime suspicion. Thus Trotsky's testimony is being used for discrediting Stalin. *Pro captu lectoris habent sua fata libelli.*

This adventitious use of the book makes it the more necessary to attempt its criticism as a historical document, and nothing else. Imagine that Danton, after his conviction, had been given a lease of life which enabled him to write a biography of Robespierre. His evidence would certainly have influenced posterity's judgment on Robespierre. Yet it is doubtful whether posterity would have accepted that evidence wholly as it stood.

Such an analogy—if an imaginary one—is as imperfect

[1] This review of Trotsky's *Stalin* appeared in *The Times Literary Supplement* on 17 July 1948.

as any comparison drawn between two real and historic situations. Stalin is, and is not, the Robespierre of Bolshevism. In the actual making of the revolution his role was incomparably slighter—the title of the Russian Robespierre goes not to Stalin but to Lenin. It is in the post-revolutionary era that Stalin has loomed just as large as, or even larger than, Robespierre; he has even combined his traits with those of the First Consul. On the other hand, Trotsky's resemblance to Danton will hardly be disputed. Both represented the same type of revolutionary leadership, oratorical genius, and tactical brilliance. Both gave expression to the whole *élan* of a revolution so long as popular enthusiasm was its chief motive force and both suffered eclipse when that enthusiasm ebbed away.

If, at times, Stalin appears to combine some traits of Robespierre with some of Bonaparte, in Trotsky also two characters at least seem to have blended—Danton's and Babeuf's. Only a few years after his resounding triumphs the universally acclaimed tribune of the people was already the hunted leader of a new Conspiracy of Equals, raising the cry for the regeneration of the revolution and defying the implacable builders of a half-revolutionary and half-conservative empire. The tide of history ran against Trotsky as powerfully as it had run against Babeuf.

What Trotsky's publishers have now produced is not a biography but an indictment of Stalin. It is a book that bears all the marks of the tremendous nervous pressure under which its author lived his last tragic years. When he wrote it he had behind him more than ten years of a frustrating isolation from the world, ten years in the course of which he wandered uneasily, in constant danger of sudden death, from one uncertain asylum to another. He was oppressed by the nightmare of the Moscow purge trials, in which he had been depicted as the centre of a most sinister conspiracy. All his children had died in mysterious circumstances which led him to believe that they had fallen victims to Stalin's vengeance. Finally, while he was still working on this book, on 20 August 1940, he was struck down by an assassin, who presumably was carrying out a verdict passed in Moscow. Only the first seven chapters were finished by him. The others were pieced together from his notes and edited, though not always in strict accordance with Trotsky's trend of thought. Trotsky would have protested against Mr. Malamuth's phrase, 'the trend towards centralization, that sure precursor of totalitarianism' or against his description of Marshal Pilsudski as 'Poland's Liberator'. Small wonder, therefore, that this posthumous book lacks the sweep and brilliance which distinguished his monumental *History of the Russian Revolution*. As a piece of writing it is disappointingly inchoate and at times incoherent. Even so, it must be said that many of its pages are illuminated by flashes of genius, epigrams, and sayings that may go down to history:

'Of Christ's twelve apostles [says Trotsky on page 416, referring to the purge trials] Judas alone proved to be a traitor. But if he had acquired power, he would have represented the other eleven apostles as traitors, and also all the lesser apostles, whom Luke numbers as seventy.'

And this is how Trotsky sums up his indictment of Stalin:

'"*L'Etat, c'est moi*" is almost a liberal formula by comparison with the actualities of Stalin's totalitarian régime. Louis XIV identified himself only with the State. The Popes of Rome identified themselves with both the State and the Church—but only during the epoch of temporal power. The totalitarian State goes far beyond Caesaro-Papism, for it has encompassed the entire economy of the country as well. Stalin can justly say, unlike the *Roi Soleil*, "*La Société, c'est moi*".'

In the conflict of the two men, principles, ideas, and policies were at stake; but the conflict of temperaments was not less important. Two so extremely contrasting personalities would have clashed in any party, in any circumstances. Stalin's mind is shrewd, strictly practical, cautious, and pedestrian. Only in an atmosphere overcharged with revolution like that of Tsarist Russia could so cautious a mind as his be attracted by the Marxian doctrine. Where his actions have the sweep of the boldest social experimentation they reflect less the qualities of that mind than the extraordinary pressures of a revolution which compel a most circumspect leader to jump over precipices, in a neck-breaking manner. As a rule, Stalin makes such jumps *contre-cœur*, when the situation in which he finds himself allows neither retreat nor advance by any normal way. Thus in many ways this most adventurous of contemporary statesmen at heart fears and abhors adventure. His inclinations are those of the stickler for the 'middle of the road', for 'safety first', even though events have consistently thrown him off the middle of the road, now towards one and now towards another most unsafe extreme. Feared by conservatives as the very embodiment of revolution, he himself has been a conservative in the revolution.

Not so Trotsky. Revolution was his proper element. He had been drawn to it by his temperament and outlook. The dialectical philosophy, which views life as the continuous conflict of opposites, continuous change and movement, was to him not merely a doctrine to be intellectually absorbed—it permeated his instinctive behaviour. While Stalin distrusts generalizations, Trotsky was in constant search for them. Stalin may often miss the wood for the trees. Trotsky had little or no interest for trees that would not make a wood. There is no end to such contrasts. Stalin shows an absolute lack of artistic sense and imagination; he relies exclusively on his solid mechanics of power. In Trotsky the artist was as strong as the political leader; he is obviously sincere when he confesses in his autobiography that he 'felt the mechanics of power as an inescapable burden rather than as a spiritual satisfaction'. He was ebullient, eloquent, generous, and picturesque, while Stalin's main characteristics are cool reserve, taciturnity, and suspiciousness. Trotsky was the *émigré* steeped in Western European culture, while Stalin breathed the air of Russia only. Small wonder that from their very first personal contact there was suspicion between them. Trotsky recalls the 'yellow glint' of animosity which he noticed in Stalin's eyes during their first conversation in Vienna, in 1913. From the beginning he treated Stalin with the contempt that he never abandoned for a moment while he was writing this book.

Trotsky's bitterness towards Stalin is unlimited. Yet the statement that bitterness too often directed his pen must be qualified. As a historian and biographer, Trotsky treats facts, dates, and quotations with almost pedantic conscientiousness. Where he goes wrong is in the constructions put on the facts; he errs in his inferences and guesses. Not rarely his evidence is based on dubious hearsay. To this category belongs his dark, vague, and self-contradictory suggestion that Stalin, in his striving for power, may have speeded up Lenin's death. Yet the historian's conscience, as a rule, does make him draw a clear line of distinction between the facts and his own constructions and guesses, so that the discriminating reader is able to sift the enormous biographical material and form his own opinions.

English readers may find the book's method of exposition extremely wearisome, repetitive, and pedantic. The author delves with unrelenting suspicion into every detail of his adversary's life. Armed with a formidable array of quotations and documents, he polemizes at great length. He often expresses agreement or disagreement with Stalin's other biographers, many of whom hardly deserve to be taken seriously, and it is pathetic that this great political and literary warrior should turn all his big guns on the hares and rabbits roaming the field in front of him.

He was not, however, writing his book with an eye to any English-speaking, or other Western, public. Nor was he greatly interested in its immediate success. Rather, in his thoughts, he addressed a Russian public whom he hoped his words would eventually reach, not, perhaps, in his lifetime: a new Russian generation inured from its cradle to the cult of Stalin and brought up on histories of the revolution, from which Trotsky's name and all that it stood for had been carefully expunged. It was for the benefit of this generation that he set out, step by step, to destroy the Stalinist cult, to reassert his own role in the revolution, and to restate what he regarded as the pristine principles of Bolshevism. The future will show whether his labour was lost or not. In ten or twenty years his *Stalin* may become a great spiritual experience for the Russian intelligentsia, a stimulus for some sweeping, unpredictable 'transvaluation of values'. A new Russian generation may find in Trotskyism (side by side with an obviously conservative and quixotic attempt to put the clock of Russian history back to 1917) a starting-point for a new trend of ideas, just as the progenitors of French socialism found such a starting-point in Babeuf.

Nevertheless, the weakness of Trotsky's indictment is not difficult to see. It appears clearly in, for example, the following passages from page 336:

'This fundamental dissimilarity [between Stalin and the Fascist dictators] is illustrated . . . by the uniqueness of Stalin's career by comparison with the careers of . . . Mussolini and Hitler, each the initiator of a movement, each an exceptional agitator, a popular tribune. Their political rise, fantastic though it seems, proceeded on its own momentum in full view of all, in unbreakable connection with the growth of the movements they headed. . . . Altogether different was the nature of Stalin's rise. It is not comparable with anything in the past. He seems to have no pre-history. The process of his rise took place somewhere behind an impenetrable political curtain. At a certain moment his figure, in the full panoply of power, suddenly stepped away from the Kremlin wall, and for the first time the world became aware of Stalin as a ready-made dictator. . . .

'The current official comparisons of Stalin to Lenin are simply indecent. If the basis of comparison is sweep of personality, it is impossible to place Stalin even alongside Mussolini or Hitler. However meagre the "ideas" of Fascism, both the victorious leaders of reaction, the Italian and the German, from the beginning of their respective movements, displayed initiative, roused the masses to action, pioneered new paths through the political jungle. Nothing of the kind can be said about Stalin.'

These words, written while Russia was entering into the second decade of planned economy—i.e., several years after the collectivization of twenty-odd million farms—had a sufficiently unreal ring even eight or nine years ago; today they sound fantastic. Trotsky's view of Stalin is coloured by the familiar but unwise contempt of an original thinker and man of letters for a greyish, dullish but yet very powerful man of action. Trotsky underrated his adversary so much that he came to see Stalin's figure, like a *deus ex machina*, 'suddenly stepping away from the Kremlin wall, in the full panoply of power'. But Stalin did not come to the fore like that. It is clear from Trotsky's own revelations that ever since the October Revolution Stalin was one of the very few (the three or five) men who exercised power; and that his practical, though not ideological, influence in the ruling group was second only to Lenin's and Trotsky's.

It was not only Stalin's personality which Trotsky underrated. He underrated also the depth and strength of the social developments which had brought Stalin to the fore, though he himself had been the first to interpret those very developments to the world. He viewed Stalin as the leader of a 'Thermidorian reaction' from the revolution, the chief of a new bureaucratic hierarchy, the originator of a new nationalist trend epitomized in Socialism In One Country. Throughout the 'twenties and the 'thirties he blamed Stalin's leadership for all the defeats that communism suffered all over the world. In these criticisms there was truth, especially in his devastating criticisms of the Comintern's policies in Germany on the eve of the Nazi era. But the sum total of his charges betrays a degree of 'subjectivism' in Trotsky which is at cross-purposes with his Marxian method of analysis. In his conception Stalin appears almost as the demiurge, the evil demiurge, of contemporary history, the one man whose vices have dominated the fortunes of international revolution. At this point Trotsky's polemics smack less of Marx than of Carlyle.

Was Stalin the leader of the Soviet Thermidor? In France the Thermidorian reaction put an end to the Terror. It did not undo the economic and social work of the revolution, but it brought that work to a stop. After Thermidor no major change occurred in the social structure of France as it had been so far wrought by the revolution. The political power moved from the *plebs* to the *bourgeois* Directory. In Russia, however, the social revolution did not come to a stop with Stalin's rise to power. On the contrary, its most comprehensive and radical acts, the expropriation and collectivization of all individual farmers, the initiation of planned economy, took place only after Stalin's ascendancy.

There is much more truth in Trotsky's other charge that Stalin came forward as the leader of a new bureaucracy which had risen above the people. Against the rigid, totalitarian outlook of Stalin's hierarchy Trotsky invoked the programme of Soviet democracy—i.e., of government by the revolutionary people—which the Bolsheviks had advanced when they seized power. Here the precedent of his argument is unmistakable to the historian: under the Directory Babeuf advocated the return to the Jacobin Constitution of 1793. However, government by the revolutionary people was as impossible in Russia in 1925 or 1930 as it had been in France in 1797. The revolutionary masses had spent their political energy in the civil war and played out their role. The 'heroic' phase of the revolution had given place to weariness and apathy; the nation's progress could no longer be prompted by impulses coming from below, but only by direction from above. So far the analogy between Stalin's régime and the Thermidorian reaction is correct.

What Trotsky understated was the extent to which the change from 'Soviet democracy' to 'bureaucratic control' had occurred in the Leninist period. He distinguishes between the two phases of the revolution, but is reluctant fully to admit connection between them. It is true that Leninism was essentially non-totalitarian; but it is also true that by the end of the civil war (say, 1920 and 1921) it had, under the pressure of events, gradually, gropingly, almost unconsciously evolved towards totalitarianism. The birth of Bolshevik totalitarianism can be traced, with a high degree of precision, to the Tenth Congress of the party in 1921. It was on the foundations laid by the 1921 congress that Stalin built up his régime in later years. Both Lenin and Trotsky thought of going back to a more democratic order; but it may be doubted whether, even if Lenin had lived longer, they would have been able to do so. Leaving aside the contemporary fascist counter-revolutions, which have been predominantly political in character and totalitarian *a priori*, no historic social revolution— Cromwellian, Jacobin, or Bolshevik—has escaped the phase of 'totalitarian degeneration'.

It is the main count in Trotsky's indictment that Stalin gave up world revolution for Socialism In One Country. To non-Marxists the dispute over this point between Trotskyism and Stalinism looks like a scholastic squabble, even if the heads of many Bolshevik leaders have rolled in the course of it. Yet, it was more than that. What in fact divided the two antagonists was not that the one 'wanted' and the other 'did not want' world revolution, but a fundamental difference in their estimate of the revolutionary potential of the working classes in the Western countries.

Underlying Trotskyism was the firm belief that at least Europe was 'ripe for socialism'. This was the thesis that had been enunciated by Karl Kautsky, the 'Pope' of international social democracy, at the beginning of the century. From this standpoint the Russian revolution was the prelude to a far wider upheaval. In Trotsky's eyes the achievements of Socialist construction in Russia alone ranked little in comparison with the grand crescendo of material prosperity, cultural advance, and spiritual freedom which could be expected from a socialist economy based and planned on a European scale. Trotsky was convinced that European capitalism had lost its vitality, and that, at heart, the European working classes were willing to give up the meretricious benefits of reformism in favour of revolution. Wherever the capitalist order succeeded in achieving a measure of stabilization, either by means of fascist surgery or by mild reformist cure, the blame, in Trotsky's eyes, lay on the shoulders of communist or social democratic leadership. He often argued that even were the victory of socialism in Europe still to be remote, it was nevertheless closer than the achievement of a truly socialist, classless society in 'backward, uncivilized' Russia. He regarded Russia as upon a periphery of modern civilization. That periphery, to be sure, contained a powerful force; it was the pioneer of socialism. But eventually the forms of the new society would not be forged upon the periphery but in the centre of modern civilization.

Upon this aspect of affairs Stalin has never formulated his mind very explicitly. First he lacks Trotsky's gift for the exposition of ideas; but, more significantly, his attitude marks a departure from Marxian tradition. Thus his real, though quasi-esoteric view, has merely been implied in his doctrine of Socialism In One Country. He never shared Trotsky's optimism concerning Europe's 'ripeness' for socialism, but estimated the powers of resistance left in the capitalist order as, on the whole, still very formidable. In the many crises of international politics between the wars—e.g., the British crisis of 1926, the rise of Nazism in Germany, the Popular Front in France, and the civil war in Spain—Stalin was much less sanguine than Trotsky regarding the receptiveness of the working classes to the ideas of proletarian revolution. To Stalin his peculiar brand of socialism in Russia was, and still is, of incomparably greater importance than the possibility of socialism in the West. He declined to regard Russia as existing upon a peripheral area of modern civilization, and was confident that Russia was destined to become the citadel of the new socialist civilization. It was Stalin's plan to build up and safeguard that citadel, even if the means used for that purpose clashed (as, for example, the Russo-German pact of 1939), or seemed to clash, with the interests of foreign working classes. While Trotsky thought in terms of a double impact, first of Russia upon the West and then of the socialist West upon Russia, Stalin sees in Russia's one-sided impact upon the West the primary and decisive factor in the fortunes of communism or socialism.

The doctrines of Trotsky and Stalin both view contemporary history as a worldwide rivalry between capitalism and socialism, a rivalry historically as legitimate as was the old struggle between the feudal and the bourgeois systems of society. Stalin has, on balance, been inclined to rely on a peaceful development of that rivalry as allowing growth and consolidation of the Russian citadel of socialism. Trotsky laid stress upon its 'cataclysmic' forms and emphasized, especially, the 'pressure of the capitalist world', under which the edifice of

Russian socialism might perhaps collapse long before it had been completed. In addition, that edifice, built as it had been on narrow and shaky foundations in a 'backward, semi-Asiatic' country, was, in his view, so dangerously misshapen as in many respects to be a caricature of socialism.

Ever since the controversy began, nearly a quarter of a century ago, events have submitted the two antagonistic doctrines of communism to continual test. The controversy is unconcluded though it is no longer thrashed out in the ranks of communism, for Trotsky's Fourth International has been stillborn. But indirectly the tenets of Stalinism and Trotskyism are being submitted to new tests at the conference tables of international diplomacy and in the social turmoil of Europe and Asia.

On the showing of these tests, Stalin's scepticism regarding the revolutionary temper of the European working classes has so far seemed better justified than Trotsky's confidence. To be sure, that temper has as often been damped as it has been stimulated by Stalin's policies. But this is no answer to the fundamental problem. No social class with a real and significant momentum of its own will allow itself to be diverted from its essential objectives by any outside influence. If Trotsky's view that the influence of Moscow had acted as the decisive brake on European revolution were correct, it would merely testify to the relative weakness of the revolutionary proletarian element in Western Europe. Moreover, Russia can no longer be regarded today as upon the periphery of Europe. Much of Europe has, on the contrary, become peripheral to Russia. This radical shift in the international balance of power alone may be held by some to vindicate, in terms of communism, the Stalinist doctrine.

But from the standpoint of the Marxist, the Trotskyist argument has by no means been finally disposed of. There still remains the problem of Stalin's régime, on the origins of which Trotsky's posthumous work has shed keen, if one-sided, illumination. Can that régime, with its leader's implicit maxim, '*La Société, c'est moi*', really lead the Russian people to a free and classless society? Or will that régime continue, as Trotsky feared, to 'degenerate', until it turns into an unequivocal negation of socialism? Or will it, as he sometimes forecast, eventually clash with the non-communist world, seek salvation in the spread of revolution or perish? To these questions history has yet to give its answer.

MR. E. H. CARR AS HISTORIAN
OF THE BOLSHEVIK REGIME

THE publication of the fourth volume of Mr. Carr's *History of Soviet Russia* offers a welcome opportunity for a general survey of his work and for an appraisal of the place it occupies in the field of Soviet studies.

It is difficult not to begin these remarks with a reflection on the state in which the writing of the history of the Russian revolution finds itself at present.[1] It is an almost incredible fact that not a single work deserving the name of a History has yet been produced inside the Soviet Union. True, the first decade of the Soviet régime brought a vast number of valuable contributions to a History, many special monographs, and collections of documents. In the intellectual *Sturm und Drang* of that period Soviet historians initiated ambitious projects of research. This, they thought, was the first time that Marxists were going to write history in all seriousness, backed up by the resources of a great State and the abundance of all the State archives recently thrown open, and sure to find response in the intense curiosity for history which had been awakened in the young generation. When if not under such circumstances should Marxism prove its unrivalled merits as a method of historical inquiry and analysis?

However, the advent and consolidation of Stalinism cast a blight upon the whole field of historical study. The Stalinist State intimidated the historian, and dictated to him first the pattern into which he was expected to force events and then the ever new versions of the events

[1] 1954.

themselves. At the outset the historian was subjected to this pressure mainly when he dealt with the Soviet revolution, the party strife which had preceded and which had followed it, and especially the struggles inside the Bolshevik Party. All these had to be treated in a manner justifying Stalin as the Leader of monolithic Bolshevism. Later the re-writing of history extended backwards to past centuries, and outwards to the history of other countries, until Cho was degraded to be not just the dignified servant of Politics—a role to which she is well accustomed—but their slave. The verve and passion with which historians had thrown themselves on the archives found a deadly enemy in secrecy which barred access to documentation. The historians could not be allowed to inquire into the facts because free inquiry was incompatible with falsification. Finally, all the chronicles of the party and the revolution, even those written in the Stalinist spirit, were banned, until at every level of teaching, from the rural party cells to the academic seminaries, students were allowed to draw from one fount only, the *Short Course of the History of the C.P.S.U.*, that bizarre and crude compendium of Stalinist myths, written or inspired by Stalin himself.

This deterioration of historical standards was not without precedent. For a long time the French revolution fared no better with its historians. Napoleon and his Prefects and Censors kept a suspicious eye on those 'ideologues' who tried to delve into the great revolutionary drama which preceded the Empire. The security of the Empire required that a curtain should descend upon the great revolution, that its ghosts be laid, and its republican and plebeian ideas be banished from people's minds. Napoleon could afford to vent openly his antipathy for ideologies and ideologues; and so, unlike Stalin, he did not even bother to dabble with history writing. He had no need to falsify history—he suppressed it. The first histories of the revolution began to appear only during the Restoration, and they were written by the enemies of the Bourbons. Stalin, placed as he was at the head of a party proud of its *historical* materialism, could not even attempt openly to suppress the history of the revolution: all the more savagely did he have to cripple and mutilate it.

Curiously enough, none of the many Russian *émigré* groups has used its enforced and long lasting political idleness to produce anything like a history. There exists no serious Monarchist version of the revolution, no Cadet version, no Menshevik account, and no social revolutionary interpretation. The White Guards produced their accounts of the civil war, among which Denikin's five volumes are still the most important, despite all their lack of sophistication. Miliukov wrote his *History* in the heat of the civil war; but it was little more than an inflated pamphlet indicting all anti-Cadet parties; and Miliukov himself was too great a scholar not to realize this. In the Preface to his work he virtually disavowed as a historian the account of events which he had given as a leader of his party. Nor have the Mensheviks, among whom there were more gifted writers and theorists than in any other *émigré* group, made any notable historical contribution. The apologetic books by Kerensky and Chernov contain no serious attempt at a reconstruction of the historical process; and even Dan's posthumous work *Proiskhozhdenie Bolshevisma* offers a certain interest as a retrospective self-criticism of Menshevism but not as a History. To all these parties and groupings involved in the struggles of 1917 the revolution was such an unmitigated disaster and their role in it appeared to themselves so incongruous and inexplicable that their theorists and writers preferred not to return as historians to the scene of those struggles. A notable exception is Trotsky's *History*, which alone transcends the limitations of apologetic writing and is a lasting literary-historical monument to 1917.

Nor can Western historiography be proud of its achievements. This is so not merely because *wer den*

D

Dichter will verstehen muss ins Dichters Lande gehen, although it will certainly be the Russians themselves who, after they have recovered from the intellectual slump of the Stalin era, will eventually write the ·great and revealing histories of the revolution. The failure of Western historians to produce an adequate interim account has also been due mainly to preoccupation with current politics. Western historiography has rarely been guilty of wholesale falsification, but it has not been innocent of suppression of facts. It has as a rule shown little or no insight into the motives and minds of the social classes and political parties and leaders engaged in the Russian struggle; and most recently the cold war has had almost as blighting an effect on research as had Stalinism itself.

It is Mr. Carr's enduring and distinguished merit that he is the first genuine historian of the Soviet régime. He has undertaken a task of enormous scope and scale; and he has already performed a major portion of it. He views the scene with the detachment of one who stands if not *au-dessus de là mêlée*, then at least *au-delà de la mêlée*. He wishes to leave his readers with understanding and he searches for both the facts and the trends, the trees and the wood. He is as austerely conscientious and scrupulous as penetrating and acute. He has a flair for seeing the scheme and order of things and is lucid in the presentation of his findings. His *History* must be judged a truly outstanding achievement.

To be sure, Mr. Carr has been able to use only such sources as have long been available to students: he has had no access to unpublished documentation. But from these admittedly limited sources he has been able to extract the utmost; and to weave it into a close textured narrative. For the period he has covered so far the published documentation is indeed so abundant and reliable that it is doubtful whether archives, when they are opened, will compel the historian to revise fundamentally the view which can be formed now on the basis of materials already published. This, incidentally, is my own experience with the Trotsky Archives which I have studied at Harvard. These contain a great number of important documents, and their knowledge causes me to disagree with Mr. Carr on certain specific points. But on the whole these disagreements, in so far as they concern the facts, are not fundamental.[1] It may therefore be assumed that Mr. Carr's study of Soviet Russia up to 1924 is as definitive as any historical work can be.

Mr. Carr is a historian primarily of institutions and policies, of which he traces the origins and the development in minute detail. He shows the Soviet State *in statu nascendi*; and this he does with a masterly grasp. But he is preoccupied primarily with the State, not with the nation and society behind it. Moreover, his interest is focused on the very top of the State machinery so that it might be said that his *History of the Soviet Union* is primarily a history of its ruling group. In part this is unavoidable: a historian reconstructs the historical process on the basis of documentary evidence which emanates mostly from the rulers, although in the years of the revolutionary upheaval Soviet society was by no means amorphous and inarticulate as to form merely a mute background. But this characteristic of Mr. Carr's work is also in part due to his basic approach. Whenever he refers to developments in the social background, his references are subsidiary to his analysis of what was going on inside the ruling group. He tends to see society as the object of policies made and decreed from above. He is inclined to view the State as the maker of society rather than society as the maker of the State.

This approach creates *a priori* certain difficulties for the historian of a revolution, because a revolution is the breakdown of the State and demonstrates that in the last resort it is society which makes the State, not vice versa. Mr. Carr approaches the revolutionary upheaval with

[1] The importance of the Trotsky Archives for the years after 1924 is incomparably greater.

the mind of the academic scholar interested above all in constitutional precepts, political formulæ, and machinery of government, and less in mass movements and revolutionary upheavals. His passion is for statecraft, not for 'subversive' ideas. He studies diligently the subversive ideas but only in so far as they may provide a clue to the statecraft of the triumphant ex-revolutionists. If he had chosen to epitomize his work in some epigrammatic motto he might have opened his *History* in the Churchillian manner with the following text: 'How Russian Society Collapsed Through the Folly and Ineptitude of its Old Ruling Classes and Through the Utopian Dreams of Bolshevik Revolutionaries, and How These Revolutionaries in The End saved Russia by Giving up Their Quixotic Delusions and Learning Arduously and Painfully the ABC of Statecraft.'

This approach is reflected even in the composition of Mr. Carr's work. The major part of his introductory volume deals with Bolshevik Constitution making, which seems to me to have been the least important, the most shadowy, aspect of the story. Another major portion of the same volume is devoted to 'policy, doctrine, machinery'; and still another, by far the best, describes the 'dispersal' of the Tsarist Empire and its 'Reunion' under the Soviet flag. What is lacking almost completely is the social background of 1917. To the academic scholar steeped in the study of Constitutions, this is of course the most natural line of approach, but it is not one which is best suited for the study of a society in the throes of revolution. As he proceeds with his work Mr. Carr progressively overcomes the limitations of this approach to quite a remarkable extent. By an almost heroic, self-critical effort of his analytical mind, he has come much closer to the understanding of the strange phenomenon of the Russian revolution than his starting-point allowed to expect. But that starting-point is still reflected in his treatment of the subject and underlies much of his reasoning.

Mr. Carr has been censured by academic critics for his attitude towards Leninism and his alleged worshipping of Lenin. One of the critics has remarked that Lenin occupies in his work the place which Caesar holds in Mommsen's History. This criticism seems to me groundless. Mr. Carr is too sceptical, too acute, and too strongly aware of Lenin's inconsistencies to be his worshipper. What is true is that in his presentation Lenin's figure dominates and overshadows the revolution, the Bolshevik Party, the Soviet State. It does so in part because of the inadequate picture of the social background, and in part because Mr. Carr is not sufficiently aware of the formative processes by which Lenin's political thought was shaped and of the extent to which, even in the years of his mature leadership and ascendancy, Lenin's mind was formed by his environment and influenced by the ideas of his followers. In this respect Mr. Carr's work suffers from a certain lack of political and psychological insight.

But what is more important is that Mr. Carr's 'apotheosis' of Lenin applies to Lenin the statesman and the self-taught master of statecraft as distinct from the Marxist revolutionary and thinker. It is the Lenin who *builds* a State that evokes his admiration, not the one who *overthrows* a State, and certainly not the one who obstinately *dreams* about the eventual 'withering away' of the State of his own making. Mr. Carr views the story of Lenin the revolutionary as the indispensable prelude to Lenin the statesman, and he has little more than a polite smile of condescending irony for the Lenin who, at the summit of power, still had his gaze fixed on the remote vision of a classless and Stateless society. Yet these different and seemingly conflicting aspects of Lenin's personality were so closely integrated that neither of them can be isolated and understood in isolation. To the reader of Mr. Carr's *History* it must remain something of a puzzle how Lenin came to achieve the stature of statesman which Mr. Carr ascribes to him.

Did he perhaps even as builder of a State find his strength in the resources of his revolutionary thought and dream?

By implication, and sometimes explicitly, Mr. Carr answers this question in the negative. He is impressed by those features which Lenin may have had in common with, say, Bismarck, rather than by those in which his affinity with Marx, the French Communards, or Rosa Luxemburg shows itself.

Reading Mr. Carr's pages I could not help thinking of a confession once made by an eminent Polish liberal publicist Konstanty Srokowski, who knew Lenin during the latter's stay in Cracow before the First World War. Having spent much time with Lenin, arguing about politics and social affairs and playing chess, Srokowski confessed later that in 1912–14 he regarded Lenin as a well-meaning but utterly impractical man with no chance whatsoever to make any impact on practical politics. 'Whatever subject we approached,' Srokowski related, 'Lenin would begin with expounding one of the tenets of Marxist philosophy. He never stopped quoting Marx as if he deluded himself that he had found in Marx's writings a master-key to all problems preoccupying mankind. I could only shrug shoulders. It was interesting to argue with Lenin for he was a man of intellect and education. But he seemed to me a quixotic visionary. I was sure that every one of our minor socialist politicians and trade union leaders was superior to him as *a man of action*. When I then learned that the same Lenin was the leader of a revolution and the head of a great State I was dumb-founded. I lost confidence in my judgment. How, I wondered, could I have committed so cardinal an error in appraising the man. There must have been something wrong in my approach to him and to politics in general.' The old Polish publicist had, of course, an exaggerated respect for practical politics and all too little regard for 'revolutionary romanticism'. Sometimes I wonder whether Mr. Carr's view of Lenin would have been any different, if he had met Lenin, say, in 1912? Essentially it is not very far removed from that view even in the *History* where it is only Lenin the successful master-builder of Soviet Russia who seems to redeem in Mr. Carr's eyes Lenin the revolutionary dreamer.

It is not difficult to detect that Mr. Carr has formed his view of the Bolshevik revolution, at least partly, in opposition to the outlook of Western diplomacy in the years of the anti-Bolshevik intervention. The generation of Western diplomats which witnessed the rise of Bolshevism and resisted it with all its might was notoriously incapable of comprehending the phenomenon against which it struggled. Mr. Carr may be described as an intellectual expatriate from that diplomacy—a rebel criticizing its tradition from the inside, as it were. We know of no other man of Mr. Carr's background who has proved capable of even a small part of that enormous mental effort which Mr. Carr has made to grasp the inner logic of Leninism. Even so, the peculiar limitations of the diplomatic mind can sometimes be sensed between the lines of his *History*.

Watching the earthquake of the Russian revolution, Mr. Carr surveys the landscape to see what has happened to so familiar a landmark as the Russian Ministry of Foreign Affairs. He is puzzled, bewildered, and worried by its disappearance. He cannot believe that the breakdown of diplomacy, brought about by the revolution, can serve any useful purpose, or that it can last. And he is relieved to find that when the dust settles diplomacy and its landmarks seem to be back where he expected them to be. The rare moments when he gives vent to irritation with the Bolshevik leaders are those in which he relates their initial hostility towards conventional diplomacy and their indulging in 'the illusion that foreign policy and diplomacy were no more than an evil legacy of capitalism'. The Bolshevik Utopians could well reply that they were forced to take up diplomacy only because the 'evil legacy of capitalism' was much heavier than they had feared. If one views the prospect of an international socialist society as utterly unreal, and if one sees the future of mankind as a perpetual rivalry between nation-States, then, of course, one must consider diplomacy, its institutions and its procedures, to be inseparable from the history of mankind. The Leninists believed that the national diplomacies of our age would one day appear as anachronistic as the diplomacies of the particularist, feudal and post-feudal, princedoms appear today; and that the unifying historical process which had merged those particularist entities into nation-States would eventually merge nation-States into an international community which will have no use for diplomacy. Mr. Carr will have none of this nonsense, and he is glad to get away from it, and to applaud generously the Bolsheviks when, like repentant prodigal sons, they give up their 'haughty contempt for the ordinary conceptions and procedures of foreign policy' and reopen a normal chancellery. Of this he repeatedly speaks as of the 'normalization' of Soviet policy, although what may seem normal by one standard may be highly abnormal by another.

How self-revealing is, for instance, Mr. Carr's description of the scene of Trotsky's departure from the Soviet Foreign Office on the conclusion of the Brest Litovsk Treaty. 'The fiery revolutionary agitator was succeeded by a scion of the old diplomacy whose early [?] conversion to Bolshevism had not effaced a certain ingrained respect for traditional forms. . . . After Trotsky's whirlwind career at Narkomindel, Chicherin sat down to a patient and less spectacular task of organization.' This contrast between Trotsky, the fiery agitator, and Chicherin in whom the virtues of the conventional diplomat had survived despite his Bolshevism, is somewhat dubious. Chicherin was as unconventional a Bohemian as one can imagine; and he was anything but a patient organizer. Trotsky, on the other hand, was in personal behaviour and habits much less eccentric than Chicherin; he easily switched from fiery revolutionary agitation to the most correct diplomatic negotiation; and he was certainly a patient organizer. Nor would the suggestion be well-founded that Chicherin's influence came to supersede Trotsky's in the conduct of Soviet diplomacy. Mr. Carr is aware that Chicherin was a mere executor of the Politbureau's decisions on which, in so far as they concerned diplomacy,. Trotsky's influence was second only to Lenin's or equal to it. We now know from the documentary evidence in the Trotsky Archives that it was Trotsky who in 1920 strove, much more insistently than Lenin, for British-Soviet agreement, for peace with Poland, for a normalization of Russia's relations with the small Baltic States;[1] and Mr. Carr himself relates some of the preliminaries to the Rapallo Treaty from which it is clear that he was also one of the chief inspirers of Rapallo, probably its chief initiator. But this scene of Trotsky's departure and Chicherin's arrival, drawn with such unmistakable relish, illustrates a conception according to which the Soviet regime gained its *raison d'être* only when it discovered its *raison d'état*.

I do not intend to deny that there was an element of unreal dream in Bolshevik attitudes or the subsequent reassertion of the concepts and procedures of traditional government and diplomacy. But how we view these is a matter of proportion and evaluation; and my criticism applies to Mr. Carr's overemphasis on the Bolshevik return to the conventional concepts and procedures and to his inadequate grasp of the revolutionary ethos of the epoch.

Mr. Carr is a great respecter of policies and—sometimes—a despiser of revolutionary ideas and principles. Again, this shows itself even in the composition of his monumental work. He relegates the ideas and principles of Bolshevism to Appendixes and Notes, treating them implicitly as points of only marginal interest, while his narrative is concerned primarily with policies. In Volume I he deals with Lenin's Theory of the State in

[1] See I. Deutscher, *The Prophet Armed*, pp. 461–71.

a Note, whereas one-third of the volume is devoted to constitution-making, although Soviet constitutions were honoured mainly in their breach and had little practical significance. Another Note deals with the 'Doctrine of Self-determination'. In the second and the third volumes the Appendixes deal with the Marxist attitude towards the peasantry and the Marxist view of war. Yet these views and ideas were active and crucial elements in the developments described in the main body of the *History*, because they animated its characters. Mr. Carr is, of course, familiar with the Marxian saying that an idea, when it gets hold of human minds, itself becomes a power. Historical realism cannot therefore consist in playing down the power of ideas, for this can only narrow and impoverish the historian's perspective.

The validity of this criticism can be illustrated by Mr. Carr's treatment of the inner Bolshevik controversy over the Peace of Brest Litovsk. His account of this is disappointing. Other writers, who lack Mr. Carr's scholarship and ability, have rendered this momentous episode with much greater insight and sense of drama. This is not mainly or even primarily a question of literary style. The Brest Litovsk controversy may be seen as a clash between political expediency and revolutionary idealism in which expediency gains the upper hand. This is a simplified but essentially correct view; and it is the one adopted by Mr. Carr. But he grasps much more acutely the arguments of political expediency than the motives of revolutionary idealism; and he is not quite sensitive to the full force of the conflict between the two. Moreover, his predilections lead him astray as a historian: he describes accurately and in great detail Lenin's arguments for peace, but he omits to give even a bare summary of the views held by the opponents of peace, who, as he knows, at first had behind them the majority of the party and repeatedly outvoted Lenin. Had Mr. Carr given a little patient attention to Bukharin's, Radek's, Yoffe's, and Dzerzhinsky's views, he might have found in them more than mere enthusiastic flamboyance and revolutionary phrase-mongering, of which there was admittedly no lack; he might also have found considerable realism and far-sightedness. Even if this should not be so, his omission to give an adequate idea of the arguments of the Left communists results in a curious gap.

On several occasions Mr. Carr refers sarcastically to the Bolsheviks' 'Wilsonian' 'appeal from wicked governments to enlightened peoples'. But was that appeal so quixotic as Mr. Carr suggests? Was it so impractical even from the viewpoint of the analyst of power politics? After all, the victorious revolution was nothing else but one great appeal 'from a wicked government to an enlightened people'. Because of his contempt for that appeal, Mr. Carr misses the revolution's climate, its emotional atmosphere, its mass enthusiasms, its moral tensions, the high flights of its hopes, and the deep depressions of its disillusionments, all of which derived from the ardent belief of both the revolutionaries and the people in the reality of that 'appeal'. Sometimes Mr. Carr's characters seem to move through an airless space and an emotional vacuum as if they were nothing but disembodied political conceptions and formulæ. In part this is due to the author's preoccupation with scientific history writing, which to him seems to imply the exclusion of the emotional and spiritual colouring of the events. As an historian Mr. Carr superbly surveys and scrutinizes his period, but he does not re-live it. Perhaps he does not consider it important and necessary or even admissible for the historian to do so. His approach has certainly its justification and validity: there are at least several legitimate ways of writing history, although the best histories are those that are works of imaginative insight and art as well as of science. But even within Mr. Carr's approach and style his insight would have gained in depth if it had not been held in check too strongly by his impatience with Utopias, dreams, and revolutionary agitation.

Mr. Carr is fascinated by the subtlety and flexibility
with which Lenin adjusted his policies to events and
circumstances. Sometimes, however, he magnifies the
element of the opportunist in Lenin out of its real proportion and to the exclusion of other elements. Lenin, the
Marxist, appears rather dimly in his pages. Mr. Carr is
not sufficiently aware of the strength of the Marxist
tradition in Lenin. When he does refer to that tradition
he seems out of his depth and makes curious errors of
fact. (Thus he claims that Lenin based in part his
Imperialism on R. Luxemburg's *Accumulation of Capital*,
which is patently incorrect. Lenin's *Imperialism* was
entirely based on Hilferding's *Finanzkapital*; and Lenin's
own economic thought, from his earliest writings to his
final evaluation of Rosa Luxemburg's ideas after her
death, was strongly opposed to Luxemburg's theory.)
What Mr. Carr describes as the 'Wilsonian' element in
Leninism was indeed part and parcel of the Marxist
internationalist tradition; and Mr. Carr, misled by the
outward similarity of some Wilsonian and Bolshevik
slogans, tends to overlook the realities behind the slogans
and the different and incompatible trains of thought from
which political watchwords had sprang. Implicitly, Mr.
Carr treats the early Bolshevik internationalism as a
purely ideological conviction, unrelated to the economic
trend of the epoch, if not simply as a sentimental weakness. Marxists had always argued that the needs of
capitalist development had been the main motive power
behind the formation of nation-States; and that one of
the central 'contradictions' of capitalism consists in the
fact that the productive forces of modern society out-
grow their national frameworks. According to this view,
the conflict between the productive forces and the
nation-State manifests itself in various forms: negatively
—in the imperialist search for *Grossraumwirtschaft*; and
positively, in the internationalist outlook of the proletarian revolution, which cannot settle down within the
framework of any nation-State.

Stalinism neglected and then suppressed this aspect of Marxist internationalism and it sought to elevate the isolation of the Russian revolution to a virtue and a theoretical principle. For all his conscious effort to resist the insinuating influence of the Stalinist way of thought, Mr. Carr unwittingly sometimes views Marxism through the Stalinist prism, because his interest in Marxism is only secondary to his study of the Soviet State. But Stalinism itself carried with it its own self-refutation for in its last expansive phase it bore reluctant but conclusive testimony to the conflict between the development of the productive forces of Soviet Union and its national boundaries. Yet, the habits of thought associated with Socialism In One Country, habits formed and consolidated in the course of a quarter of a century, persist; and they colour the thought even of a student as critical and detached as Mr. Carr. In the heyday of Stalinism it may have looked as if Bolshevik internationalism had no more economic and historic substance behind it than had the abstract cosmopolitanism of the French revolution (to which Mr. Carr indeed relates it). But at present it should no longer be possible to take this view: it is more than clear that the Russian revolution, unlike the French, has initiated not just a new type of the nation-State, but—for good or evil—a new and expanding international economy and society.

The vantage point from which history is written is of great consequence. It would have been natural for an historian of Mr. Carr's background to treat the early Bolshevik internationalism as Wilsonian and Utopian in, say, 1932, although even then this would not have been proof of great historical realism. But it is a positive anachronism to treat it so twenty years later. In the retrospective light of the Chinese revolution and of the expansion of Stalinism in Eastern and Central Europe, the early Bolshevik hopes for the spread of revolution appear to have been tragically ahead of their time, but by no means Utopian.

Perhaps the main weakness of Mr. Carr's conception is that he sees the Russian revolution as virtually a national phenomenon only. He does not deny its international significance or its impact on the West. But he treats it as an historical process essentially national in character and self-sufficient within the national framework. He thinks in terms of statecraft and statecraft is national. His Lenin is a Russian super-Bismarck achieving the Titanic work of rebuilding the Russian State from ruin, and of re-uniting its dissolved component parts. This view is correct and incorrect at the same time—it misses the broader perspective within which Lenin's achievement places itself.

A Lenin shorn of his unmanageable revolutionary internationalism and shown as master of national statecraft may appear plausibly as nothing but Stalin's legitimate ideological forebear. In the *History* Mr. Carr has done very much to reconstruct the authentic picture of Leninism and to free it from Stalinist accretions. He has succeeded admirably in his presentation of facts which is, on the whole, irreproachable; but he has only half succeeded in some of the finer shadings of emphasis and interpretation. Unwillingly he overdraws those features through which Lenin may be seen as resembling Stalin and he blurs the others in which the dissimilarity and contrast are striking. Here, too, I would like to qualify the criticisms and to add that Mr. Carr's understanding of the subject deepens with the progress of his research; and that in this respect, too, his latest volume, *The Interregnum*, represents a notable advance. When he reaches the threshold of the Stalin era, Mr. Carr is much more aware of the discontinuity between Leninism and Stalinism than he was while he analysed Leninism.

This is perhaps the most difficult and complex problem by which the student of the Soviet Union is confronted. The historian's mind grappling with this issue inevitably oscillates over the years; and as a fellow-worker in the same field I do not claim to have struck any faultless balance between the factors making for the continuity and the discontinuity of Leninism and Stalinism. Unlike the Stalinists, the Trotskyists, and the vast majority of the anti-communist writers, for whom this problem does not even exist, Mr. Carr comes to grips with it. To the Stalinist Stalin is the legitimate heir to the apostolic succession of Marx-Engels-Lenin. To the Trotskyist he is the traitor, grave-digger, and rene-gade of Leninism. The great majority of anti-communist 'Sovietologists' also see in Stalinism a straight con-tinuation of Leninism, while a minority accepts the Trotskyist version because it is polemically so conve-nient to denounce Stalinism as a devilish betrayal of the 'true' communism as well as a menace to Western values. Each of these schools is trading in half-truths, and refuses to face the fact that in some respects Stalinism is the 'legitimate' development of Leninism, while in others it is its negation. Mr. Carr's work is free from such simpli-fications and half-truths; but it nevertheless still seems to overdraw the Stalin in Lenin.

This inclination induces Mr. Carr to antedate certain trends in Soviet foreign policy and to project back the Russian traditionalism of Stalin's diplomacy on to Lenin's conduct of foreign affairs. The antedating is noticeable in several instances, into which I cannot go here; but it is most striking when he surveys the Rapallo Treaty and the preliminaries to it—there he unwittingly injects the flavour of 1939 into the situation of 1921-2 and tends to treat Lenin as the straight precursor of the Stalin who was to share out Polish spoils with Hitler. Mr. Carr sees an 'ultimate alliance between Bolshevik Russia and a Germany of the Right' as an historic in-evitability manifesting itself in both situations. 'Assum-ing that the Bolshevik régime survived, such an alliance would give the Reichswehr what it would one day need —a free hand against the West; and it would also give German heavy industry its indispensable market' (Vol. III, p. 310). The argument about the market cuts both ways, to say the least: twice within a quarter of a century German heavy industry backed not an alliance but an invasion of Russia in order to obtain control of that 'market' or, to put it more accurately, of Russian and Ukrainian sources of raw materials. Superimposing the pattern of 1939 on 1921–2 Mr. Carr suggests that the Rapallo Treaty was directed against Poland and that underlying it was the perennial Russo-German striving for Poland's dismemberment. That the idea of Poland's dismemberment with Russian help lured the German Right even in 1920–2 is true, of course; but it is not true that it evoked any response in Soviet diplomacy or in the Bolshevik leadership of the Lenin era.

Indeed, nothing would show better the gulf between two phases of Soviet diplomacy than a careful comparison between Rapallo and the Nazi-Soviet pact. In both pacts Russia strove to strengthen her position by 'exploiting the contradiction' between Germany and the West while the West either ostracized Russia or worked to exclude her influence from European diplomacy. But in 1922 Russia joined hands with a Germany vanquished and outlawed, not with the imperialist incendiary run amok of 1939. At Rapallo the Bolsheviks made a sober deal without compromising their principles and their integrity and dignity: there was in their whole behaviour not even a hint of that state of mind in which, seventeen years later, Molotov could send Hitler the ill-famed telegram assuring the Führer of a 'friendship cemented by blood'. And the Rapallo pact was not concluded at the expense of weaker neighbours: even in its secret parts it contained not a single arrangement made at the expense of Poland, for instance. Outwardly Rapallo and the Nazi-Soviet pact may look like two consecutive phases of the same policy; but they are set apart by the imponderable difference between the political morality of Leninism and that of Stalinism, a difference which Mr. Carr tends to overlook.[1]

[1] It is my duty to use this opportunity for explaining a curious incident in the preliminaries to the Rapallo pact. In his little book *German-*

In spite of these flaws and limitations Mr. Carr's work will remain a great and enduring landmark in historical writing devoted to the Bolshevik revolution. Its merits are so obvious that they need no further underlining in a journal for specialists. Even the criticisms made here testify to its high standard, for they could not apply to a work less distinguished than this *History* is by consistency of method and unity of approach. In the future various schools of historians will study the Russian revolution with the same interest and passion with which

---

Soviet Relations, published in 1951, Mr. Carr quoted Lenin as instructing his diplomats to 'play the Polish card' in negotiations with Germany. Mr. Carr referred to the Trotsky Archives, and quoted myself as the source of the information. I feel therefore co-responsible for this error and obliged to put it right especially because the version given in *German-Soviet Relations* has been widely quoted by other writers.

Among several documents bearing on the preliminaries to the Rapallo Treaty, the Trotsky Archives contain a 'strictly secret' memorandum addressed, on 10 December 1921, to Moscow by a cryptic German 'negotiator'. The author of the memorandum, apparently an official German personality favouring agreement with Russia, surveyed the factors which operated in Germany against such an agreement and went on to advise the Bolsheviks what counteraction they should, in his view, take in order to prepare the ground for a diplomatic deal. Among other things, he suggested that the Bolsheviks should 'play the Polish card' especially in connection with the conflict which flared up over Upper Silesia. It was that German 'well-wisher' who used the phrase about 'the Polish card', not Lenin. In all the highly confidential and illuminating documents of the Trotsky Archives relating to this episode, there is not the slightest indication that Lenin's government paid any heed to this advice. In those years the Politbureau had not yet sufficiently freed itself from 'idealistic illusions' to respond to such promptings. This was still Lenin's not Stalin's Politbureau; and its members could only contemptuously shrug shoulders over the 'playing of the Polish card'. Mr. Carr certainly does not treat as historical evidence for the opposite view the gossipy third-hand account of Enver Pasha, an adventurer-interloper who tried in vain to build himself up into a sort of a mediator between Moscow and Berlin and to whom the Bolshevik leaders made no confidences, as can be seen even from his own 'report'. In the *History* Mr. Carr himself corrects the version given in the *Soviet-German Relations*; but somehow that version still seems to reverberate in his reasoning.

the records of the French revolution have been searched for the last 130 years; and each generation and each school of historians will uncover new sources and throw new shafts of light on the great epic. But every future historian will have to turn to Mr. Carr as his first great guide as the French historian still turns to the work of Thiers, with which Mr. Carr's *History* has quite a few features in common. This comparison gives perhaps a measure of Mr. Carr's achievement.

PART THREE

———————

THE CLOSE OF THE STALIN ERA

MID-CENTURY RUSSIA[1]

I

I T is more than a hundred years since Alexander
Herzen, the great Russian rebel and exile, wrote in
his 'Open Letter to Michelet' that 'Russia is quite a
new State—an unfinished building in which everything
smells of new plaster, in which everything is at work and
being worked out, in which nothing has yet attained its
object, in which everything is changing, often for the
worse, but anyway changing. . . .'

On another occasion Herzen contrasted the outlook of
the Russians with that of the Poles. The latter, he said,
cultivated a romanticism utterly alien to the Russians.
They lived in their national past while the Russians,
finding in their past and present little that was worthy of
attachment, fixed their gaze exclusively on the future.
The thoughts and emotions of the Poles hovered mourn-
fully over ancestral graves, while Russia was full of
'empty cradles waiting for children to be born'.

Herzen's reflections must have sounded topical to
many Russians even in the middle of this century. Since
his days revolutions have followed one another; whole
classes of Russian society have disappeared or have been
liquidated; new classes have grown up or have been
forcibly brought into existence by government decree;
national institutions, beliefs, ideas, and illusions have
been destroyed and manufactured wholesale; and the
whole social and moral climate of the country has

[1] This essay is based on a series of my articles which appeared in *The Reporter* (New York) in the summer and autumn of 1951.

changed so much that it seems that even the old character and temperament of Russia has suffered complete
extinction or complete transformation. And yet mid-
century Russia was still the 'unfinished building smell-
ing of new plaster'—and of—smouldering ruins. Nothing
in it 'had yet attained its object, and everything was
changing, often for the worse, but anyway changing'.

When one thinks how many generations of Russians
have consoled themselves with the thought that their
national existence was 'an unfinished building' one may,
at moments, feel with a shudder that a Sisyphean curse
hangs over Russia's labours. This must have been the
feeling with which, in 1945–6, many millions of demobi-
lized soldiers and war-time evacuees were returning to
their homes in Western Russia and in the Ukraine. They
found their native towns and villages razed to the
ground. They found that the coal mines, the steel mills,
and the engineering plants they had built, amid blood
and tears, under the pre-war Five Year Plans, were
flooded, demolished or dismantled and carried away.
The Western provinces of the Soviet Union, where so
many gigantic battles had been fought, were heaps of
ruins; and the tools were lacking with which to clear the
ruins away. Twenty-five million people lived in mud
huts and dug-outs. And, in 1946, as if to fill the cup of
bitterness which victorious Russia was draining, a cala-
mitous drought, the worst within living memory,
scorched the fields and blighted the crops. Bled white,
half-crazy with suffering, hungry, half-naked and bare-
foot, Russia began to build anew.

A few statistical indications will show that this is not
an overdramatized description of the condition in which
Russia emerged from the war. When the last shots were
fired, Soviet industry produced less than two-thirds of
its pre-war output; and, of course, the bulk of its produce
consisted of munitions. The annual output of steel was
down to about 12 million tons, only a little more than
half the pre-war output. The factories were turning out

about 40 per cent of the clothing and footwear they used
to produce, and most of it went to the armed forces.
Even before the drought, the sugar plantations yielded
less than a fourth of their normal crop. The Soviet
consumer could not get more than one-fourth or one-fifth
of the very meagre rations of meat, fat, and milk he consumed before the war. Apathy and weariness threatened
to thwart recovery. The Politbureau strove to stir and
shake up the working class with exhortation, threat, and
promise; and a note of genuine alarm sounded in all its
appeals for higher production.

Yet five years after the surrender of Hitler's armies
Russia's recovery was well under way. The momentum
of that recovery was the most important development of
the first post-war decade. In 1945 Russia still ranked as
only the fourth or fifth among the industrial powers of
the world; in 1950–2 she was indisputably second only
to the United States. Her steel output, approaching 40
million tons per year, was three to four times as large as
it was towards the end of the war and more than twice
as large as in 1940. It was this recovery which enabled
Russia to consolidate and expand the positions of power
which she had precariously acquired through military
victory.

II

How can a nation achieve so startling an advance
within so short a time?

This is not the first time in history that a nation has
found its economic ascendancy stimulated and speeded
up by military victory. The Franco-Prussian War of
1870, for instance, led not only to the unification of the
German States under Prussia's leadership but also to the
rapid rise of Germany's modern industry. The contribution which Bismarck levied on defeated France amounted
to a transfusion of economic power from the Third Republic to the Hohenzollern Reich. The French payments
fed the orgies of financial and industrial speculation

which were characteristic for the *Gründerperiode* of the
1870's and 1880's. Up to 1870 France had been the
leading industrial nation on the Continent. She lost that
position to Germany never to recover it.

Stalin's reparation policy resulted in a similar transfusion of economic power. The dismantling and confisca-
tion of industrial plant in defeated countries, the repara-
tions from current production, the mixed joint stock
companies set up, under Russian management, in Eastern
and Central Europe, all served to transfer wealth from at
least eight countries to the Soviet Union. This policy
could not but re-kindle the hatred of Russia among her
neighbours; and it piled up before the Russian government dangerous problems and difficulties which were to
outlast Stalin. But it cannot be doubted that the policy
was a powerful catalyst of Russia's economic growth. It
deprived Germany of the rank of the leading industrial
power on the Continent with the same finality with
which Germany had deprived France of that rank after
1870.

However, important though this transfusion of economic power was, it was not decisive for Russia's
ascendancy. Turning from war to peace, the Soviet
Union found a firm and solid basis for its recovery in
those industries which it had built up in its Eastern
provinces, in the Urals and beyond, in the 1930's and
which it had feverishly expanded during the war. The
East had fed with munitions the retreating and advancing
Soviet armies; and now it supplied the sinews of reconstruction to the Western provinces. No wonder that the
Soviet East loomed very large in the mind of mid-century
Russia. Even after the rehabilitation of the western lands,
it was in the East that the pulse of the Soviet economy
beat more strongly. More than half of the industrial
plant remained in the Urals and beyond.

The tempo of post-war industrialization represented a
triumph of Soviet planning. After the economic setback
of the war, it was even more important than before that

the nation's resources should be marshalled, allocated, and used in accordance with a single national plan enforcing a severe economy of scarce materials and tools and a strict labour discipline. The techniques of planning, which had first been developed awkwardly and with many costly and even tragic mistakes in the 1930's, were now brought up to a high standard of efficiency, even though they were still hampered by bureaucratic rigidity. The theory of planning was one of those very few fields in which the general intellectual depression of the Stalin era did not prevent the achievement of definite progress. The planners had at their disposal an amazingly effective 'secret weapon': the famous theorems of 'simple and expanding reproduction' which Karl Marx had developed in the second volume of *Das Kapital*. Those theorems, modelled on Quesnay's *Tableaux Economiques*, describe the composition and circulation of a nation's productive resources under capitalism. Adapted by Soviet planners to a publicly owned economy and further developed, they helped to produce results which future historians may well describe as the most momentous feat in social technology achieved in this generation.

But the planners with their theorems would have been suspended in a vacuum without the sustained daily labour of the many millions of workers, skilled and unskilled, and of the technicians and managers. Many of the workers and managers did their work willingly and even enthusiastically, bringing into it something of that spirit of devotion and sacrifice which had enabled Russia to win the war. Few could blame Stalin's government for the ruins and for the miseries which attended Russia's victory—these were seen as the work of Hitler, not of Stalin. But there was also in the Soviet people much despondency and plain demoralization, against which the government proceeded to use the well-tested instruments of totalitarian terror. This bred new grievances and new resentments all the more poignant because the terror was applied to people whose self-confidence had been heightened through victory and who had been sustained in the ordeals of battle by the hope that post-war Russia would be a freer and better country than the Russia of the 1930's with her cruel labour codes, purges, and concentration camps. The rulers resolved to nip in the bud any incipient opposition. They resorted once again to the tightest thought-control. Once again Zhdanov came forward as the intellectual Inquisitor of the day.

III

Thus, feats of planning, enthusiasm for reconstruction and a most severe and comprehensive discipline combined to enable Russia to make the new stupendous jump ahead.

To accumulate wealth, the maximum of wealth in a minimum of time, was the overriding purpose of Stalin's policy in his last years. More coal, more steel, more machine tools! More oil wells, more railway lines, more waterways, more power stations, more atomic piles! Mid-century Russia was worked up into a frenzy of accumulation. Implacably the employer-State kept down the wages of workers, grabbed the earnings of peasants, and feverishly ploughed back its fabulous profits into the national economy.

Mid-century Russia was nearly completing 'Primitive Socialist Accumulation'. Nobody dared to utter these words, because the man who had first put forward the formula, Eugene Preobrazhensky, had been denounced and purged as a traitor and an enemy of the people. An old Bolshevik and an original theorist and economist, Preobrazhensky had, even in Lenin's last years, opposed the party's drift towards the totalitarian State, and later he joined hands with Trotsky. But, paradoxically, it was he who supplied in advance the text for Stalin's work, without suspecting for a moment to what ruthless use his theory would be put.

Marx describes as 'primitive accumulation' the ways

and means by which the early middle classes accumulated wealth in the sixteenth, seventeenth, and eighteenth centuries when modern industry was still too small and too feebly developed to expand on its own, 'legitimate' profits. The main sources of early capitalist wealth, Marx argued, were the dispossession of the yeoman-peasantry, colonial plunder, piracy, and later also the underpayment of wages. Only with the growth of industry and its productive power did the normal profits of the capitalist entrepreneur become substantial enough to serve as the main source for the further, normal accumulation of wealth. It was only then that a respectable and civilized capitalism could expand without necessarily robbing workers of their wages and plundering other classes of society.

Before the Russian revolution it had never occurred to Marxists that socialism, too, might pass through a phase of Primitive Accumulation. They had always assumed that the already accumulated bourgeois wealth, when nationalized, would serve as the basis for socialism. But there was not enough of that wealth in old Russia; and still less of it was left by the time the Bolsheviks had won the civil war and began to look to the future. When in the early 1920's Preobrazhensky expounded the idea of Primitive Socialist Accumulation he caused an uproar of Bolshevik indignation: it was still blasphemous to suggest that socialism could be built by methods comparable to those employed by early capitalism. Yet, the whole social history of Stalinism, right up to the middle of the century, was nothing but the massive and awe-inspiring epic of Primitive Socialist Accumulation. As its promoter, Stalin expropriated the private farmers, confiscated the produce of the collective farms, and kept the industrial working class, ever swelling in numbers, on a bare subsistence level.

But towards the end of his life the great pirate of socialism had done his job. Russia's new wealth had grown so enormous that it could now expand rapidly by itself, from the surplus of its own produce, by means of normal accumulation rather than by means of plundering the working classes and the peasantry. But Stalinism could not free itself from all the habits and the powerful inertia of Primitive Accumulation; and it resisted mentally the demands of a new time which called for a transition to normal accumulation.

The wealth of the nation stood in the sharpest contrast to the poverty of the people. In its main branches Soviet industry was now producing per head of the population as much as was produced, say, in France, though still less than in Britain and the United States. To see the advance in the proper perspective it is well to remember that twenty to twenty-five years earlier Russia was still much nearer in this respect to the level of India and China than to that of France. This is not to say, however, that the Soviet people enjoyed anything like French living standards. The industrial wealth of the nation consisted primarily of producer goods which were used to turn out more producer goods, and only a minimum of articles of consumption. In its frenzy of accumulation Stalinism seemed spellbound by that 'production for production's sake' in which Marx had seen the lunacy of capitalism. Under nearly all the Five Year Plans the consumer industries had failed to reach the very modest targets set to them. By 1950 there was little or no starvation; but Russia's staple diet was still bread, potato, and cabbage. The city dweller consumed hardly more than half a pound of meat in a week, one-sixth of the American consumption; and not more than a pound of fats of all sorts in a month. For clothing he had to do with about 20 yards of cotton fabric per year, while the American had 60 yards and the Briton 35; and the Soviet citizen could obtain almost no woollen fabrics, no rayon, and no nylon. Statistically he was able to buy one pair of shoes per year, while the average American bought three, and the average Briton at least two pairs.

Worst of all was the housing situation which resembled

the dismal picture of the slums of early Victorian England described by the young Engels. During a quarter of a century, between 1925 and 1950, the urban population of the Soviet Union grew by about 50 million people, as much as the whole population of the British Isles, the vast majority of the newcomers being peasants shifted from the countryside. The cities and towns had not been prepared for so formidable an influx. The housing programmes were absurdly inadequate. Stalin's upstart bureaucracy and he himself were more interested in erecting grandiose public edifices and monuments, unsurpassed in respectable banality, than in building dwellings for human beings. Under the first post-war Five Year Plan 100 million square metres of housing space was provided; but this was too little to make good even the war-time destruction of housing. The average space for every homeless or virtually homeless towndweller amounted at the most to four square yards, less than any decent farmer would allow his beast of burden. Lack of accommodation for workers threatened at times to disrupt the industrial plans. In Stalin's last years the few startling cases in which Soviet citizens dared openly to criticize Ministers were those connected with the housing scandal.

IV

While, despite all her miseries, urban and industrial Russia was forging ahead with mighty vitality, rural Russia sluggishly lagged behind. The war had robbed the farms of manpower, tractors, horses, and cattle. Yet the structure of collective farming did not collapse—it was only weakened. Much as the peasant originally resented collectivization, he now knew that there was no way back from it. The old private smallholding had been inseparable from the horse, its chief traction power. But the horse had since been disappearing from the countryside; and its place on the fields had been taken by columns of huge tractors operated by the State-owned

Machine Tractor Stations and suited for work only on large-scale farms. The first thing the government did after the war was to restore and re-equip the Machine Tractor Stations, which formed the most massive links between town and country and the instruments of the town's economic predominance. The peasant knew that he could not do without the help of the Machine Tractor Station and that he could benefit from it only as a collective farmer. But not all the economic energy of the peasantry was directed into collective channels. The *kolkhoz* remained an economic hybrid, semi-collective and semi-private. Beside the commonly owned fields there were still the residual tiny smallholdings privately owned by members of the *kolkhoz*. The peasant tenaciously clung to his smallholding, and often tried to develop it at the expense of the collective economy. He had to divide his time between the collective field and his own plot which competed intensely for his labour.

The still smouldering resentments of the peasantry and the cleavage inside every farm between its collective and its private elements accounted for agriculture's lagging behind industry. This was the most important domestic issue which preoccupied Stalin's Politbureau in its last years. If industry was to grow, farming had to feed the continuously expanding urban population; and the growth of agriculture had to be stimulated especially in the East where there were too few settled farming communities around the new industrial centres. Otherwise the whole convoy of the Soviet economy would in the end be compelled to move at a pace dictated by its slowest sector.

In 1950 rural Russia was once again in the throes of an upheaval which affected the lives of a hundred million people. In the spring of that year the government decreed a merger of farms throughout the Soviet Union. This was the most sweeping change since the initial collectivization of the early 1930's—a supplementary collectivization. At the beginning of 1950 there existed in the Soviet Union 250,000 collective farms, each with an average acreage of about 1,000 acres. By the end of the year there were only 120,000 farming units, each covering about 2,500 acres. The reform aimed at weakening or destroying what had survived of the old individualistic village. The pre-1950 collective farm was fitted into the framework of the old rural community: in most cases the peasants of one village had been organized in one collective farm. Under the supplementary collectivization not only farms but entire communities were merged. The Politbureau hoped that the enlarged farms would be more efficient and easier to control and manage.

The peasantry accepted the merger with reluctance, but without any of that desperate resistance with which it had fought against the initial collectivization. It mattered little to the peasant, at least immediately, whether the collective fields he tilled belonged to a smaller or a larger *kolkhoz*. And the memories of the pitiless suppression of the rebellion of the early 1930's were still alive and discouraged new acts of resistance.

The supplementary collectivization, however, could not lead to a rapid and massive rise in agricultural efficiency. The Stalinist Politbureau was divided over policy towards the peasantry and decreed the merger of farms as a palliative. So many years after the liquidation of the various Trotskyist and Bukharinist oppositions the ghost of the old controversy still haunted the Kremlin. Some members of the Politbureau argued that in order to obtain higher crops, and a bigger output of meat and dairy produce, it was necessary to give more scope to the peasantry's repressed but still surviving individualism. This meant lower agricultural taxation, payment of higher prices for food to the peasants, and a more abundant supply of cheap industrial goods to the countryside. Other members of the Politbureau held, on the contrary, that the peasant's individualism should be curbed and suppressed even more severely than hitherto, and that collectivization should be carried to its extreme conclusion.

The country had a glimpse of the controversy when
N. Khrushchev, then leader of the Moscow branch of
the party, proposed in public that the merger of the
collective farms should be accompanied by a resettle-
ment of the rural population. The farmers, he urged,
should be shifted from their houses and huts to special
settlements, Agrotowns, which were to be built in the
centre of the new enlarged *kolkhoz*; and the *kolkhoz*
should take possession of the privately owned plots of
land which usually adjoined the farmer's old dwelling.
Khrushchev's scheme was supported by other party
dignitaries, but it was emphatically disowned by the
Politbureau. Stalin was afraid, not without reason, that
so drastic a policy would plunge the countryside in
bloody turmoil; and in his old age, beset by grave international problems, he was not prepared to start another
collectivist crusade. Nor was he willing to adopt the
alternative policy of concessions to the peasantry. True
to himself to the end, he played for time and meanwhile
he attempted to strike a balance between conflicting
policies. He was to leave his successors to grapple with
the unresolved crisis in agriculture.

V

With all her unresolved problems mid-century Russia
was the prodigy of modern history. An incredulous world
witnessed her breaking the American monopoly of
atomic energy: in 1949 it learned about the event from
an official announcement put out by the White House,
not by the Kremlin. More than anything else that event
drove home to the West the meaning of the transformation that Russia had undergone under Stalin. Who
would have believed it possible that 'backward, inefficient, semi-Asiatic' Russia should be able to overtake so
rapidly the old industrial nations of Western .Europe
and to reach the threshold of the atomic age second only
to the United States?

In 1945 it was still possible to wonder just how enduring would prove Russia's military ascendancy over Europe. It was still plausible to see in Stalin merely a modern successor to Peter the Great who had also worked ruthlessly to modernize Russia, to teach her the crafts of more advanced countries, to build up her military power, and to extend her influence abroad, but whose achievement had, on the whole, not outlasted his own reign. The flow and ebb of Russian power was familiar in a later age, too. The armies of Alexander I had marched triumphantly into Paris as Stalin's soldiers marched into Berlin. Nicholas I, the gendarme of the counter-revolution, had dictated his will to Russia's small neighbours and had treated Prussia as his vassal. But then Russia's power slumped; her armies returned home; and her influence abroad shrunk because her internal structure was too weak and obsolete to back it up. Whatever some of the Tsars had done to modernize Russia, their achievement was superficial and ephemeral: economically Russia remained the least developed of the great European powers. It was from her fitful attempts to emerge from backwardness and from her equally fitful relapses that the feeling sprang, so aptly expressed by Herzen, that Russia was for ever the 'still unfinished building', rising and crumbling and rising again and always as far from completion as ever.

At the end of the Stalin era, however, for the first time in history Russia's power rested on solid and stable industrial foundations. Stalin's achievement therefore was different in kind from that of Peter the Great. Peter the Great broke open a 'window to Europe', but he left the entire edifice of Russia rickety and backward. Stalin, on the contrary, slammed, blocked up, and blacked out all of Russia's windows to the outside world; but he rebuilt the whole edifice to its foundations, and modernized and expanded it beyond recognition. The black-out was designed to keep out all external influences that might have interfered with the work of construction

E

inside, and it prevented the builders from comparing their own existence with what was going on outside.

Russia's hermetic isolation from the world was a pre-condition of Primitive Socialist Accumulation. But it was carried to the most grotesque excess when Primitive Socialist Accumulation was already far advanced. Mentally trapped behind the slammed doors and windows, Russia was taught to distrust and despise the world outside, to glory in nothing but her own genius, to care for nothing but her own self-centred greatness, to rely on nothing but her own selfishness, and to look forward to nothing but the triumphs of her own power. Stalinism tried to annex to Great Russia all the feats that the genius of other nations had created. It declared it to be a crime for the Russian to entertain any thoughts about the greatness, past or present, of any other nation—to 'kowtow to Western civilization'—and a crime for the Ukrainian, the Georgian, and the Uzbek not to kowtow to Great Russia. Stalin himself, the clumsy and inarticulate yet awe-inspiring deity of mid-century Moscow, stood as the embodiment of that Great Russia, of her history, power, and genius.

VI

There can be no doubt that the enlightened elements among the Soviet people felt oppressed by the mental isolation from the world to which Stalinism subjected them; and some of them reacted with acute claustro-phobia. In fact Russia's isolation was receding into the past, and this made the self-centredness of Stalinism all the more unbearable. In the era of Socialism In One Country nothing was more natural for the Russian com-munist than to cling desperately to his solitary 'rampart of socialism'. But several smaller 'outposts of socialism' had since risen in Eastern and Central Europe; and the Chinese revolution was just erecting another gigantic rampart in Asia. The feeling of isolation could not but begin to dissolve in Russia. Yet to the end Stalinism went on to fan it, to exacerbate it, and to exploit it to the utmost.

The victory of Chinese communism did not at once make its full impact on Russia. For years Soviet citizens had read in their newspapers about obscure guerrilla fightings in various parts of China. But these stirrings of a remotely creeping revolution did not in their eyes change the picture of the world to which they had become accustomed. And when as if suddenly the Chinese revolution ceased to creep and rose for its Marathon race, and when the old order of China came down with a crash, the event was so unexpected in its magnitude as to appear almost incomprehensible and unreal.

Before the Chinese revolution most of Russia's wartime and post-war acquisitions were still tenuous. The new communist régimes in Eastern Europe were only limited and local gains; and each of those régimes might have turned out a broken reed. With Warsaw and Budapest and even Prague in communist hands, Socialism In One Country and its mentality had not yet outlived their day. But the Chinese revolution shook the world as it had not been shaken since 1917. It brought a supreme triumph to Stalinism. Yet in the cup of victory, mixed with the wine there were a few drops of poison. The rise of Chinese communism rendered ridiculous some of the Stalinist habits of mind, especially its self-centredness and self-adulation. China suddenly reopened the vistas of international revolution which had inspired Bolshevism in its early, Leninist days and which later seemed to have hopelessly faded. It was as if the ghost of early Bolshevism mocked the ageing Stalin. He shrunk convulsively and tried to pull his party even deeper into its Russian shell, into its spurious Great Russian pride and xenophobia. For a few years the deafening din of an official chauvinistic Great Russian propaganda was the only sound that came out of Russia. The mental horizon of Stalinism contracted most pathetically just when communism was achieving undreamt-of material expansion.

In a way the last years of Stalinism were as nightmarish as were its middle years. True enough, there were none of the volcanic outbursts of terror which occurred in the 1930's. On the contrary, the terror seemed to have spent much of its impetus. Up to the time of the scandal with the Kremlin doctors, that is up up to 1953, there was no unearthing of sinister conspiracies in Moscow, no hectic search for traitors and enemies of the people, no witches' Sabbath comparable to that of 1936–8. During the whole closing phase of the Stalin era only one member of the Politbureau, N. Voznessensky, the head of the State Planning Commission, was purged; he disappeared suddenly and noiselessly, without being called upon to prostrate himself and confess his crimes in public. Other party members charged with heresy or deviation suffered mild demotion but escaped the extreme forms of punishment. Yet the outward surface of Soviet life was more monotonous and more deadly uniform than ever before; and it was this its unrelieved monotony that was almost as excruciating as were the bloody spasms and convulsions of the 1930's. With the Stalin cult at its dizzy height, with all thought stagnant and congealed, it looked as if Russian history had come to an uncanny standstill. This was, of course, an optical illusion: the appearance of stagnation concealed an intense movement.

VII

Late in the last century Frederick Engels wrote about the United States:

The Americans may strain and struggle as much as they like, but they cannot discount their future—colossally great as it is—all at once like a bill of exchange: they must wait for the date on which it falls due; and just because their future is so great, their present must occupy itself mainly

*with preparatory work for the future, and this work, as in
every young country, is of a predominantly material nature
and involves a certain backwardness of thought. . . .*

Engels' words could *a fortiori* be applied to Russia at
the middle of this century. The contrast between her
material progress and the backwardness of her thought
was her most striking characteristic. Yet the most
idealistic elements of Soviet society could not but 'strain
and struggle' in muteness, and try to 'discount' their
'colossally great' future. Once again they fixed their
gaze on the vision of that future, on those 'empty cradles
waiting for children to be born' which Herzen had seen.

The only relatively free debate which occurred in mid-
century Russia was concerned with the 'transition from
socialism to communism'. To outsiders this was bizarre
scholastic quibbling over esoteric dogma; and this in
part it was. But to those engaged in it the dispute offered
an occasion for dreaming aloud, dreaming about the day
when the nightmares of the present would dissolve,
when the State with its all too familiar terrors would
wither away, after all, when the social inequalities of the
Stalin era would be overcome, and when the mastery of
man over man would become a memory of the past.

No other modern nation has been as creative and as
tragically wasteful of energies, men, ideas, and dreams
as contemporary Russia. At mid-century her birth-rate
was probably higher than that of almost all other Western
nations; so was her mortality. Even before the war, for
every child born in New York more than two were born
in Moscow. But for every funeral in New York there
were nearly two funerals in Moscow. The Russians were
consequently an astonishingly young nation. But throughout the Stalin era, the young people had little time to
enjoy the taste of youth; very early they had to shoulder
the burden of grim maturity, and they grew old with
frightening rapidity.

This was symbolic of the Stalinist way of life and of the production of material and spiritual wealth. The government had made the people build thousands of factories and mines under a single Five Year Plan. Then thousands of factories were destroyed or burnt down through war, hundreds of mines were flooded, scores of cities were razed, and flourishing lands were turned into deserts. Thousands of new schools and scores of universities were opened under each Five Year Plan; and, at great expense to society, a generation of educated and intelligent people was brought up of which the most civilized nation would be proud. Yet a terribly high proportion of that new intelligentsia was swallowed by concentration camps opened simultaneously with the universities. The brains of those who escaped this lot were flattened and stultified by the bureaucratic machine which absorbed them. At mid-century 37 million people were being educated at Soviet schools of various grades. This achievement did the greatest credit to a people many of whom had lived in illiteracy until recently; and in any case it was an encouraging promise for the future. But how many of those who received their education could be confident that they would be allowed truly to serve society with their brains?

No nation in the last century was as productive as Russia of epoch-making ideas, world-embracing Utopias, and momentous revolutions. Yet nowhere were ideas, Utopias, and revolutions so cruelly perverted. But the fertility of the Russian mind was by no means exhausted. In ideas, as in population, the balance of the high birthrate and the high mortality remained unknown.

And there were a multitude of empty cradles all over the place.

'SOCIALIST COMPETITION'[1]

I

THE economists and theorists of all socialist schools of thought agree in the denunciation of capitalist competition and of its laissez-faire apologists. But behind this unanimity in denunciation can be discerned wide differences in approach and argument, differences which finally come into the open when any socialist school tries to look beyond capitalist society and to answer the question whether socialism itself is compatible with any form of competition. The different answers given to this question reflect broader differences between the various visions and conceptions of socialism.

Perhaps the most crucial theoretical controversy over this subject took place between Marx and Proudhon more than a century ago. Proudhon saw socialism essentially as a 'free association' of small property owners, of independent producers owning their means of production. It was natural for him to envisage the economic activity of such a society in terms of competition. The evil of capitalism, Proudhon argued, was that it gave the banker and the industrialist a monopoly on the means of production and thus degraded the small artisan and peasant into wage-slaves. Under such conditions, genuine competition, which presupposed the equality and the freedom of those taking part in it, was impossible. The form which competition had taken under capitalism was therefore the Hegelian antithesis of free association and co-operation. Socialism would break the capitalist monopoly on the means of production; it would restore to the

[1] *Foreign Affairs*, April 1952.

individual the tools of his labour; and thereby it would also restore competition to its proper role. From a factor of social disruption and distintegration, competition would become a factor of harmony; and socialism would represent the final synthesis between association and competition. 'Competition', Proudhon wrote, 'is as essential to labour as is division of labour . . . it is necessary for the advent of equality.' It is inherent in human nature, and therefore 'there can be no question of destroying competition, a thing as impossible to destroy as liberty; we have only to find its equilibrium. . . .'

Marx's approach was essentially historical. He replied to Proudhon's argument with the assertion that pre-capitalist society knew little or no competitive economic activity. The feudal landlords had been engaged in all sorts of political and military rivalry; but, as a rule, they had not confronted one another as economic competitors, buyers or sellers, because their economy had not developed in terms of market relationships. Nor had the peasant serfs (or the slaves in economies based on slave labour) competed with one another as labourers. Only as market relationships had spread and become universal, i.e. under capitalism, did every form of economic activity assume a competitive aspect. Even capitalism was not always competitive. In its mercantilistic beginnings it was monopolistic. Only with its growth and consolidation, and with the development of modern industry, did monopoly give place to free trade and competition. But then free competition itself, progressively concentrating wealth in the hands of the few, tended towards monopoly. Competitive economic activity was thus characteristic only for a relatively short period in man's history; and from that period Proudhon mistakenly projected it into the past and the future.

Marx did not question the assumption that the urge for emulation was inherent in human nature. He merely insisted that this urge ought not to be confused, let alone identified, with economic competitiveness. 'Competition is emulation for profit.' Since, in contrast to Proudhon, he saw socialism as the abolition of property, not a new redistribution of it, and as a free association of producers collectively owning their means of production, not as an association of small property owners, Marx could see in socialism no room for profit and, consequently, no room for 'emulation for profit'. 'Socialist competition' was to him a contradiction in terms; and he ridiculed Proudhon's view about 'the eternal necessity of competition'.

Of special relevance to the subject of this article is Marx's view of competition as it affects the working class, that is, of competition among the workers themselves. In one of his earliest works, *The German Ideology*, he wrote: 'Competition makes individuals, not only the bourgeois but *still more so the workers*, mutually hostile, in spite of the fact that it brings them together. It takes therefore a long time before these individuals can unite.' The worker appears on the market to sell his labour force, which has become a commodity. On the labour market he competes against other members of his class; and this competition is governed by the law of supply and demand. When the market is against him, the worker cuts the price of his peculiar commodity, agrees to work for lower wages and longer hours, and compels other workers to do likewise. The competition rages inside the factory and workshop as well—competition in intensity and productivity of labour; and at the bench as on the labour market the brutality of the competition depends on the size of the 'reserve army of unemployed'. Through trade unionism the workers may restrain and curb their own competition, but they cannot abolish it. The whole social and political development of the industrial working class is nothing but a constant struggle of that class to keep down the economic individualism of its members and to impose on them solidarity *vis-à-vis* the employers.

'The separate individuals form a class', continues Marx, 'only in so far as they have to wage a common battle against another class; otherwise they are on hostile terms with each other as competitors.' Only in so far as the workers overcome their own competitiveness and grow aware of their deeper and broader antagonism to the capitalist class do they begin to act as *eine Klasse für sich*, a class for itself. Nevertheless, under capitalism they can never quite escape the curse of competition. No matter how strong their trade union, every slump tends to destroy or to weaken their hard-won solidarity. And throughout all the phases of the trade cycle competition goes on inside the factory and the workshop; and each form of wages has a different effect on it. Time wages appear to be less detrimental to the workers' solidarity than piece wages, for although they may induce some men to work longer hours, they do not induce them to outdo their fellow-workers by greater intensity of labour within any time limit. Piece wages, on the other hand, play much more strongly upon the worker's competitive instinct. 'Since the quality and intensity of the work are here controlled by the form of the wage itself,' Marx writes in *Das Kapital*, 'the piece wage automatically registers the slightest difference in the quality and intensity of the work performed.' It 'tends to develop on the one hand the individuality of the worker and with it the sense of liberty, independence and self-control of the labourers, on the other—their competition with one another. Piece work has, therefore, a tendency, while raising individual wages above the average, to lower this average itself. . . . *Piece wages is the form of wages most in harmony with the capitalist mode of production.*'[1]

Neither Marx nor Engels, nor any of their eminent intellectual disciples such as Kautsky, Plekhanov, or

[1] The italics are those of the present writer. Incidentally, Marx carefully distinguished between 'productivity' and 'intensity' of labour. Higher productivity comes with improved machinery and better organization of labour; it may or it may not indicate increased exploitation. Higher intensity of labour comes from the greater physical exertion to which piece wages spur on the worker—it nearly always amounts to increased exploitation.

Lenin, has ever drawn any blueprints of the society of the future. At most they all deduced certain general features of socialism by inference from the opposite. They assumed, expressly or implicitly, that economic phenomena which they saw as being peculiar to capitalism would vanish with capitalism or would not, at any rate, survive into the age of fully-fledged socialism. Wages, profit, and rent represented such social relationships, peculiar to capitalism and unthinkable in socialism. The same was true of the modern division of labour, especially the separation of brain work from manual labour; and, last but not least, of competition.

Marxist theory takes it for granted that the members of a socialist community will have to perform certain functions in many ways similar to those performed by their ancestors under capitalism or feudalism. In every social order men have to produce in order to live. In every economic system there must be some balance between production and consumption. Every society, if it is not to stagnate and decay, must produce a surplus of goods over and above the sum total of the goods necessary for the upkeep of the producers, the maintenance and replacement of productive equipment and so on. Yet the social relationships within which these functions are performed are so different in various systems that it is useless to search for common historical and sociological denominators for these functions. The surplus produce of a capitalist economy takes the form of rent, profit, and interest; and this determines the entire mode of life of the capitalist world. In socialism, the surplus produce, belonging to society as a whole, would cease to be profit. The function of that surplus and its impact upon social life would be altogether different from what it was under the old order, when the scale and the rhythm of any nation's productive activity were normally determined by whether that activity was or was not profitable to the capitalist class. In the same way, the emulation in which men would engage under socialism (or communism) would have little or nothing in common with their ancestors' competition. Under capitalism, men compete for profits or wages. Socialist emulation would be economically disinterested.

It is perhaps important to remember the major premise of this argument. In original Marxist theory, communism (or socialism) is associated with a development of mankind's productive resources and capacities superior to that achieved under capitalism at its peak. Marx and Engels held that man cannot make his leap 'from necessity to freedom', from 'pre-history into history', or for that matter from competition to emulation, as long as he has to devote the major part of his creative energy to the satisfaction of his material needs. Unlike some socialist sentimentalists, the founders of the Marxist school had no quarrel with the familiar view that the higher achievements of our culture and civilization have been essentially the work of the 'leisured classes'. But they believed that the time was not very far off when technological development would enable mankind as a whole to become a single 'leisured class', as it were, provided mankind could in time achieve a new social organization. In Marx's age the average working day in industry was twelve hours; and Marx hailed the introduction of the ten-hour day in England as the first great victory of the socialist principle. To most of his contemporaries the idea of a six- or seven-hour day appeared as fantastic as that of a two- or three-hour day may appear now. Yet, some Americans at least will perhaps agree that if the United States were merely to maintain the rate of its technological progress (and on condition that this progress does not become a factor of destruction and self-destruction), the two- or three-hour day should come within the realm of the possible for the American people before this century is out.

What are the implications of such a hypothesis? What would a two- or three-hour working day mean to the American people? It would certainly revolutionize their way of life and their outlook to an almost unimaginable extent. It would in the first instance render obsolete the inherited division of labour, especially the separation of brain work from manual labour. It would leave the physical worker with enough leisure for him to be free to acquire the education and to engage in the intellectual or artistic activity which under the present division of labour is open to the brain worker only. On the other hand, even the most specialized scientist and artist could easily perform physical labour for two or three hours without thereby being diverted from his special intellectual pursuit.

It was some such society as this hypothetical American society of the end of the twentieth or the beginning of the twenty-first century that Marx and Engels had before their eyes when they discussed the various phases in the development of communism. Only in this light can one understand, for instance, the following passage, almost bursting with optimism, from Engels' *Anti-Dühring*:

'In making itself the master of all the means of production, in order to use them in accordance with a social plan, society puts an end to the former subjection of men to their own means of production. *It goes without saying that society cannot itself be free unless every individual is free.* The old mode of production must therefore be revolutionized from top to bottom, and in particular the former division of labour must disappear. Its place must be taken by an organization of production in which, on the one hand, no individual can put on to other persons his share in productive labour, this natural condition of human existence, and in which, on the other hand, productive labour, instead of being a means to the subjection of men, will become a means to their emancipation, by giving each individual the opportunity to develop and exercise all his faculties, physical and mental, in all directions; in which therefore *productive labour would become a pleasure instead of a burden.*' (Italics those of the present writer.)

Only in such a society, holding a modern industrial

cornucopia, did Marx and Engels expect that productive labour could become a disinterested sports-like social activity and that competition could give place to emulation.

To most reform-minded socialists and trade unionists these Marxist vistas of the future have always seemed either too unreal or too remote to be taken very seriously. The romantic undertone in Marxism has evoked a response in the revolutionaries, as Lenin's *State and Revolution* strikingly testifies. The reformists have tried more empirically to find a compromise between capitalism and socialism; and they have tended to project that compromise on to the future, at least on those rare occasions when they have not shied off from generalizations about the future. Thus, the English Fabians imagined that socialism would inherit most economic 'categories' from capitalism and 'remodel' rather than abolish them. They believed that workers' competition, i.e. their competition for material rewards, would be both useful and necessary to a socialist economy, as John Stuart Mill had pointed out even before the Fabians. But while Fabian ideologists were anxious theoretically to infuse competition into the future socialist order, the trade unionists, who have directly or indirectly drawn inspiration from them, have been concerned mainly with eliminating or mitigating workers' competition under the existing order. The trade unions of most countries have at one time or another bitterly opposed the advance of 'scientific management and organization of labour' and the introduction in industry of such innovations as the stopwatch, the man-record chart, and so on. Before the First World War, the American Federation of Labour vehemently denounced the attempt of employers to drive the workers into scientifically organized, 'suicidal' competition in the factory shop. The A. F. of L. then rallied its following to resist the onslaught on their class solidarity, the onslaught led by Frederick Winslow Taylor. American trade unionism seems long since to have made its peace with 'scientific management'; but the old battle-cry of the A. F. of L. was taken up in Europe, and there it has resounded for decades. Throughout the 1920's and 1930's Taylor and Taylorism were to the European worker synonyms of the worst capitalist exploitation. In this opposition to 'technical rationalization', the defence of the worker's interests and the fear that scientific organization of labour would result in an increase of redundant labour have inevitably been blended with an instinctively conservative attitude towards technological progress. The more limited a country's resources, and the fewer its chances for economic expansion and rapid absorption of redundant labour by new industries, the more acute has been the workers' fear of their own competitiveness.

II

Any labour party, Marxist or non-Marxist, social democratic or communist, revolutionary or reformist, finds this traditional attitude untenable as soon as it assumes office. In this one respect there is little difference between Lenin and Trotsky and Attlee and Cripps. Very soon after the Bolshevik revolution Lenin tried to impress his party with the crucial importance of industrial productivity and with the need to raise the discipline and efficiency of labour. Without hesitation he recommended to his followers 'the adoption of much that is scientific and progressive in Taylor's system, the correlation of earnings and output'.[1] He further urged his adherents to try out the effect of piece wages upon the workers and their productivity, although at the same time, in March 1918, he proposed that the new programme of the party should provide for the 'gradual levelling out of *all* wages and salaries in *all* occupations and categories'. He encouraged the introduction of piece

[1] Cf. *The Next Tasks of the Soviet Regime*. Lenin's Menshevik critics bitterly attacked him more than once for urging the Russian workers to imitate the methods of American capitalism.

work and piece wages with some caution, as an experiment; and he went on to insist on the régime's basic commitment gradually to reduce the inequality of wage- and salary-earners. He also placed great emphasis on the value of emulation, which was to develop 'in humane not in zoological forms'. He interpreted emulation rather broadly:

'The problems on which emulation in the communes, associations of consumers and producers, and in the soviets ought to centre . . . are these: in which commune, in which part of a city, in which factory, in which village are there no hungry people, no unemployed ones, no rich idlers . . . where has more been done to raise the productivity of labour, to build new and good homes for the poor or to house them in the mansions of the rich? Where has most been done in order that every child in a poor family should get its bottle of milk?'

There was little emphasis in all this on competition between individual workers for higher output and higher wages. Lenin returned to the idea of emulation in 1919, when he wrote on the so-called *Subbotniki*, groups of workers, communist railwaymen, who, at the height of the civil war, volunteered to do special shifts of work during weekends in order to help to supply the Red Army. The *Subbotniki* started an 'emulation'; and they received and expected no pay at all for their weekend shifts. Lenin extolled their enthusiasm and disinterestedness and remarked that the example given by them pointed by way of anticipation to the socialist emulation of the future. This was an incident in the building up of communist morale during the civil war rather than a pronouncement on economic policy; and the incident would not perhaps have been worth mentioning had it not been for the fact that Stalinist publicity for the latter-day brand of 'socialist emulation' uses Lenin's words on the *Subbotniki* as its text. As we shall see later, the 'socialist emulation' of the Stalinist era has little in common with its alleged precedent.

During the civil war (1918–20) and in the years that followed, Lenin did not specifically resume his advocacy of 'Soviet Taylorism'; and this was no matter of chance. Scientific management and organization of labour are meaningless unless they are applied to a more or less orderly economic environment, in which at least the even flow of raw materials and equipment to the worker is assured and the worker's basic needs are more or less satisfied. None of these conditions existed then. The Russian economy had utterly disintegrated; industry was cut off from raw materials; industrial plant was half-destroyed or rotting; and the industrial population was starving—in Moscow and Petrograd the worker's daily food ration often consisted of one-eighth of a pound of bread and a few potatoes. It was an extraordinary achievement for the Soviets to wrest from this disintegrated economy the munitions, the food, and the clothing which the Red Army needed. The achievement was due to a set of emergency policies which came to be rationalized and idealized into the system of 'war communism'. There was no lack of emulation among groups of Bolshevik enthusiasts; but there was little talk as yet about *socialist* emulation. Despite all the familiar illusions of war communism, the Bolshevik leaders were aware that this idealistic emulation was not characteristic of the economic climate of the country. Amid the appalling poverty of those years, the prevalent form of 'emulation', a form in which the vast majority of the people engaged, was black-market competition.

Only towards the end of the civil war, when the Soviet leaders began to prepare for the economic transition to peace, did they make a new attempt to tackle the problem; but the attempt was still made in terms of war communism. Trotsky, hesitantly supported by the Central Committee of the party, was the chief author of the economic policy of that period, a policy which consisted in militarization of labour, labour armies, and 'socialist emulation'. He submitted to the Ninth Congress of the party (1920) the following resolution which was adopted:

'Every social system . . . has its own methods and ways of labour compulsion and education for labour in the interest of the exploiting classes.

'The Soviet order is confronted with the task . . . of developing its own methods, designed to raise the intensity and efficiency of labour on the basis of a socialized economy and in the interests of the whole people.

'On a par with the propaganda of ideas, which should influence the mind of the toiling masses, and with repressive measures, to be used against deliberate idlers, drones and disorganizers, emulation is the most powerful means towards raising productivity of labour.

'In capitalist society emulation had the character of competition and led to the exploitation of man by man. In a society in which the means of production have been nationalized, emulation in labour ought, *without impinging upon the workers' solidarity*, only to raise the sum total of the products of labour.

'Emulation between factories, regions, shops, workshops, and individual workers should be the object of careful organization and attentive research on the part of the trade unions and the economic administration.' (The italics are those of the present writer.)

To this day these words are quoted in the U.S.S.R., without their author ever being mentioned, as a sort of a Magna Carta of Stalinist 'socialist emulation'. Trotsky was aware of the dilemma implied in his appeal. He insisted that emulation should not 'impinge upon the workers' solidarity', that it should not, in other words, 'degenerate' into competition. But how was this to be achieved? In the hypothetical communist society of the future the contradiction was to resolve itself automatically. Amid an unheard-of abundance of goods, collectively produced and owned, the producers' interest in the material rewards would gradually wither away. Men would no longer wrest from one another the necessities, and perhaps not even the luxuries, of life. Only then would emulation and solidarity become fully compatible. But how could they be made compatible at the early stages of the transition from capitalism to communism, in a country whose economic resources were then, and were to remain for decades, greatly underdeveloped? Trotsky placed qualified trust in the nationalization of the means of production as a safeguard against the recrudescence of the old competition among the workers. But was this an adequate safeguard? Years later, Trotsky himself remarked with disillusioned sarcasm that by itself 'State ownership of the means of production does not turn manure into gold'. Nor could it by itself transform competition into emulation.

In the last year of war communism, Trotsky in his turn appeared before the Russian workers as the chief advocate of Soviet Taylorism. He had to consider whether the Russian worker could be persuaded to accept Taylorism or whatever was to pass under that name, and not to expect special material rewards for individual efficiency. Could 'scientific management and organization of labour' make progress, without using wages policy as its instrument? Trotsky hesitated. Alternately he advocated the adoption of incentive wages and the equalization of wages. Lenin was quick to point to Trotsky's inconsistency: 'You cannot have emulation, i.e. inequality in production,' he argued, 'without admitting inequality in consumption.' But 'inequality in consumption'—differential wages—tended to undermine the workers' solidarity. The 'gold' of socialist emulation was turning into the 'manure' of bourgeois competition.

On the eve of N.E.P., Lenin, at any rate, was clearsighted enough to see that the Russian economy could not be rebuilt, and that the next step towards socialism could not be made, without the reintroduction of a strong element of ordinary bourgeois competition, including competition between workers. But as a Marxist theorist, Lenin was also scrupulous enough not to label this 'socialist emulation'. Thus he who early in 1918 had first sketched in public statements and more extensively in private notes the prospects of socialist emulation was in later years more reticent on this subject than almost any Bolshevik leader.

After the introduction of N.E.P. in 1921 little or nothing was heard about emulation during nearly a decade. During the major part of this period the Soviet economy had to contend with vast industrial unemployment; and neither the workers nor the trade unions nor even the party were in a mood to work out the Soviet version of Taylorism.

Only in 1929, at the beginning of the first Five Year Plan, was the call for socialist emulation raised again. It was Stalin himself who raised it; and he did so without any of the theoretical or socio-political scruples that had inhibited the leaders of the earlier period. He was embarking upon the industrialization of the U.S.S.R. with the conviction that he had to foster among the workers the most intense competition in productivity and that he had to offer them, together with persuasion and coercion, the attraction of incentive wages. He was determined to unleash 'bourgeois' competition among the workers; but he was also bent on labelling it 'socialist emulation'. With characteristic vigour and crudity he stated in May 1929:

'Emulation is the communist method of constructing socialism on the basis of the utmost activity of millions of toilers. . . . Socialist emulation and competition represent two altogether different principles. The principle of competition is defeat and death of some competitors, the victory and domination of others. The principle of socialist emulation is that the advanced workers should render comradely assistance to those who lag behind in order to advance together.'

This oversimplification served a definite purpose. The 'principle' of competition is, of course, not 'the defeat and death of some and victory and domination of others', although this may be the result of competition. Its principle is, as Marx put it, emulation for material reward. Stalin banished this plain and incontrovertible definition from Soviet economic thinking in order that the new régime introduced in industry together with the Five Year Plans—the régime of shock work, Stakhanovism, and of sharply differentiated incentive wages—could be invested with the halo of socialist emulation. At the Sixteenth Congress of the party (1930) Stalin went even further: 'The most remarkable feature of emulation', he stated, 'is that it brings about a basic change in people's views on labour, that it transforms labour from a drudgery and a heavy burden ... into a matter of honour, a matter of glory, a matter of bravery and heroism.' The more brutally he shifted his practical emphasis towards material rewards (and other methods in which there was neither honour nor glory nor heroism), the more did Stalin's 'ideological' propaganda describe his labour policy in terms of the ultimate communist ideal.[1]

Whatever the ideological embellishments, the 'bourgeois' competition which Stalin fostered in the Soviet

[1] That Stalin and the Politbureau had their reasons for surrounding 'Socialist competition' with ideological embellishments is understandable. This helped them to break down the original resistance to competition inside the Party, in the trade unions, and among rank and file workers. What is much more strange is the assiduous credulity with which the ideological embellishments were sometimes accepted at the face value by outsiders. The Webbs, for instance, devoted a whole chapter of their *Soviet Communism* to the reproduction of all the myths on Socialist emulation. They surpassed themselves, however, in the following incongruous passage:

'The pleasurable excitement of Socialist emulation was actually brought into play in 1931-3 among the tens of thousands of convicted criminals, "politicals", and *kulaks* employed, as we have already described, on the gigantic civil engineering works of the White Sea canal. Brigade competed with brigade as to which could shift the greatest amount of earth, lay the greatest length of rail or construct the greatest amount of embankment within the prescribed period—sometimes, it is recorded, refusing to stop work when the hour for cessation arrived, in order to complete some particular task."

working class was to a large extent both necessary and useful to Soviet industry. This is not the place to try to summarize Soviet labour policy under planned economy —I have recently attempted to do this in a monograph on the Soviet trade unions. Suffice it to say here that in the last decade or so before the Second World War the industrial working class of the U.S.S.R. expanded so rapidly that it grew from about 10 to nearly 35 per cent of the Soviet population. This growth was interrupted by the war, but it has continued again since 1945–6. The bulk of the new labour force—24 million people under the pre-war Five Year Plans—has been recruited from the rural population. It has had to be given some elementary, hasty industrial training; and a relatively numerous section of it has had to be trained into skilled and efficient workers. The government has had an obvious interest in gradually raising the efficiency of this vast and ceaselessly expanding mass. For this a comprehensive and elaborate system of incentive wages has been needed. Piece wages, that classical stimulant of workers' competition, became the dominant form of payment in Soviet industry. Already towards the end of the 1930's about 75 per cent of all Soviet workers were paid piece rates; and their proportion has grown since, while the rates have been ever more and more differentiated. This alone gives a measure of the competitive climate prevailing in the Soviet factory and workshop.

The 'socialist emulation' of the 1930's and 1940's represented only a primitive though broad approach by Soviet industry towards Taylorism and kindred versions of scientific management and organization of labour. No doubt some technologically advanced concerns and establishments carried out complex experiments in this field throughout this period. But in most sectors of Soviet industry the rhythm of technological advance was at first too slow and then too uneven and jerky, the labour force too raw and management too much hampered by political and bureaucratic interference for any systematic scientific organization of labour to be practised over most of these years. Only recently has there been evidence of a more genuine attempt to apply Soviet Taylorism more or less on a mass scale. Specialized Soviet periodicals discuss this attempt in a tone suggesting that Soviet management is breaking completely new ground. On closer analysis it seems that, despite all claims to originality, the U.S.S.R. is essentially still in the imitative period in this field, trying hard to adopt methods which have long been familiar elsewhere. The stopwatch and the man-record chart are still startling innovations. Undoubtedly, they do mark an important stage in the growth of Soviet industrial productivity.

It is only natural that Soviet conditions should impose modifications, which make the Soviet version of Taylorism in part less and in part more effective than its American original. By and large, Soviet workers still compete for the bare necessities of life. This in itself tends to make the competition much more brutal than that to which a working class living in a capitalist country but enjoying a higher standard of living would be willing to lend itself. The fact that the Soviet trade unions, or the bodies that exist under that name, far from curbing the competition, do their utmost to spur it on, works in the same direction. Too fierce competition between workers is by no means conducive to scientific organization. Nor does the customary Soviet emphasis on quantity production, so often harmful to quality, agree with either scientific management or the rational planning of labour processes.

On the other hand, Soviet industry derives certain exceptional advantages from the circumstance that it is publicly owned and centralized. It is not encumbered by vested interests and restrictive practices. It is—or, at any rate, it should be—easy for any successful innovation in scientific organization of labour to spread, without undue friction or delay, over any sector of industry where it can be applied. Whatever other sorts of secrecy may be characteristic for the Soviets, internal commercial secrecy is not one of them. No Soviet concern or trust can have any solid motive for withholding its experience and achievements from other concerns; and the central pooling of technological and organizational experience is a decisive advantage.

In one further respect does the climate of Soviet industry favour Soviet Taylorism. The fear of unemployment never haunts the Soviet worker, whatever other fears may prey upon his mind. Restrictive craft practices are virtually unknown to him. Vertical mobility, to use the American term, is extremely high. In a society relentlessly forging ahead with its industrial revolution, to which it sets no limits, the chances of promotion open to workers are practically unlimited, or limited only by the fear of responsibility that goes with promotion. Nothing deters the skilled worker from imparting his skill to the novice and the junior at the bench; and there is much to induce and even to compel him to do so. It is one of the characteristic obligations which figure prominently in all the contracts for socialist emulation that experience in more efficient management and use of labour should be unstintingly turned into common property.

It is rather difficult to gauge the effect of the non-material incentives and deterrents which are widely employed in 'socialist competition'. The rewards of the efficient worker include official decorations, flattering publicity, social standing. The inefficient finds his name on the blackboard over the bench. Whether favourable distinction or blacklisting has the intended effect depends largely on the morale of the environment in which the worker finds himself. Among a discontented or sullen factory crew, official praise and honours are most likely to isolate the Stakhanovite. But it is impossible to say what is the prevailing mood at the bottom of the industrial pyramid. As a rule, the moral prizes go to the Stakhanovite together with the material ones; and both mutually enhance their respective effectiveness.

Finally, one more aspect of this problem, a purely political one, should be considered. We have quoted Marx as saying that 'competition makes individuals, not only the bourgeois, but even more so the workers, mutually hostile'. Marx goes on to say: 'Hence it is a long time before these individuals can unite. . . . Every organized power confronting these isolated individuals, who live in relationships daily reproducing their isolation, can be overcome only after long struggles. To demand the opposite would be tantamount to demanding that competition should not exist in this epoch of history, or that the individuals should banish from their minds relationships over which, in their isolation, they have no control.' Competition, in other words, tends politically to atomize the working class and to prevent it from organizing and using its strength for its own ends. Here is perhaps a clue—to be sure, only one of many—to the political amorphousness of the Soviet working class in the last decades, an amorphousness contrasting sharply with the political initiative, vitality, and organizing ability of the Russian workers under Tsardom. The new generation of Soviet workers has brought with it from the countryside a residual but still strong peasant individualism, upon which 'socialist competition' superimposes a new brand of individualism. Because most often the Soviet worker must fiercely compete for the bare necessities of life, his competitive individualism has certainly assumed extreme forms, making it difficult for him to develop his own political personality. Primitive economic individualism in the worker is, paradoxically, one of the essential preconditions for Stalinist collectivist uniformity, as essential as political terror, if not more so. Socialist emulation, because it is only competition under a new name—the struggle of all against all—makes the workers mutually hostile and 'isolated from one another'. They live in relationships which daily reproduce their isolation. Their energy, politically shapeless and undifferentiated, is therefore easily made to flow into moulds operated by a single party. They work and build new cities and open up deserts and fight world-shaking battles; but, like most of mankind, they are still merely the object of history. They may become something more only after long struggles. 'To demand the opposite would be tantamount to demanding that competition should not exist in this epoch of history.' Or, that the Soviet workers should 'banish from their minds relationships over which in their isolation they have no control'.

STALIN'S LAST WORD[1]

I

SHORTLY before his death, Stalin himself, in his *Economic Problems of Socialism in the U.S.S.R.*, offered a virtual survey of the social achievement of the U.S.S.R. in the Stalin era. In his own way he pointed not only to the grandeur but also to the contradictory nature of that achievement. His essay may now be read as his political testament. The following article, written and set before Stalin's death, analyses some of his ideas. One need not be a devotee of the Stalin cult to recognize Stalin's last published work as a significant political document, despite its characteristically dogmatic and scholastic style.

The Economic Problems of Socialism in the U.S.S.R. contains three different lines of argument: a statement of dogma; a survey of crucial economic and social problems; and suggestions for practical policy. All these aspects are closely interconnected, and so the survey of current problems and the suggestions for future policy cannot be properly understood without some attention being paid to the dogmatic points.

Stalin wrote his article (and the accompanying letters to various Soviet economists) in connection with a discussion which took place, in November 1951, over the conspectus of a new textbook of political economy. His remarks are devoted mainly to the treatment accorded in the textbook to the 'transition from socialism to communism'. For some time past this 'transition' has stood

[1] *Soviet Studies*, April 1953.

in the centre of theoretical argument and of day-to-day propaganda. The slogan refers back to the familiar distinction, drawn by Marx in his *Critique of the Gotha Programme*, between the 'two phases' of communism, the 'lower' or the socialist and the 'higher' or the communist proper. For many years it has been a virtual canon of Stalinism that the Soviet Union has already completed the building of socialism. Thus the problem of the transition to communism has been posed almost automatically. Recently the discussion of the ways and means and of the tempo of the transition has tended to become specific; and differences of opinion have begun to appear. In what phase of the transition does the Soviet Union find itself at present? What are the immediate prospects? In what way can the transition be speeded up and facilitated? These have been the problems under debate.

Inevitably an air of unreality has enveloped much of the discussion, if only because its chief premiss—the achievement of socialism—is itself utterly unreal. Stalin's Marxist critics have often asked how the Soviet economic system can be described as socialist when the standards of living of the Soviet peoples are notoriously low, much lower than those attained in Western capitalist countries. Is socialism compatible with growing economic inequality? Or with massive coercion by the State? Stalin has in the past done his best to evade some of these questions and to answer others in terms of the Marxist doctrine. He has argued that economic inequality is justified and unavoidable under socialism, as Marx clearly indicated when he drew the distinction between the two phases of communism. Stalin has further pointed out that the withering away of the State (that is of coercion by government), which the founders of Marxism expected, could occur only in an international socialist commonwealth, not in a single, isolated, socialist State. But Stalin and his followers have carefully avoided any realistic comparison between Soviet and foreign standards of living, because it has been politically impossible for them to admit that standards of living were and still are lower in the Soviet Union than in the capitalist West.

The claim that the Soviet Union has achieved socialism is based on the view that nationalization of the means of production and the prevalence of planned economy by themselves constitute socialism, regardless of how developed or underdeveloped are the economic resources of the country concerned, how high or low its standards of living and under what degree of State compulsion the country lives. Even in the light of this simplified definition, however, the socialist character of the Soviet economy must still appear doubtful. While Soviet industry may be said to conform to the definition, Soviet farming has, even after collectivization, represented a mixed type of economy. The land has, in strict law, been national property ever since 1917, although this legal fact has even now hardly become part and parcel of the peasantry's thinking and attitude towards the land. The Constitution and the Statutes of the *kolkhoz* guarantee eternal use of the land to the collective farms and of small private plots to individual members. The Machine Tractor Stations are owned and operated by the State. Livestock, implements, buildings are corporate or private property. The *kolkhoz* owns its crops; and after having met its obligations towards the State, it is free to sell the crops. The individual *kolkhoznik* is free to take to the market the produce of his private plot and that part of the collective crop which is allocated to him. Collective farming thus represents at best a semi-private and semi-socialist sector of the economy. Officially, however, collective farming has been labelled socialist, in order to justify the claim that socialism had been established in the entire Soviet economy.

This misrepresentation of the social aspect of Soviet farming has produced a great deal of doctrinal equivocation and 'double talk'. Stalin's article deals in fact with some of the effects of that equivocation. This is not merely a matter of dogma, for dogma impinges on practical policy and administrative experience. Since the canon about the achievement of socialism had been proclaimed, new cadres of economists, administrators, planners, and organizers have grown up. Some of them have received a thorough grounding in classical Marxist economic theory. In their minds the tenets of that theory often tend to clash with the Stalinist canon. These 'young cadres' have the advantage over the Bolsheviks of an earlier generation that they have been plunged directly from school into a vast, complicated, and rapidly expanding planned economy, where they can test academically acquired notions of Marxist theory against facts of life. Sooner or later—perhaps later rather than sooner—they may be able to enrich the theory in the light of their unprecedented experience and thus to contribute towards overcoming the present stagnation and decadence of Marxist economic thought. For the time being, however, they themselves are the victims of the bureaucratic-ecclesiastical manipulation of economic theory. Stalin now tries to free them from some ill effects of that manipulation and in his turn exposes them to new manipulation.

The young economist or administrator who accepts the canon about the socialist character of the economy is inevitably puzzled and bewildered by many aspects of Soviet policy. He wonders, for instance, why 'socialist' farms should trade their produce and why market relationships should persist under socialism? If he has read carefully the famous passage from Marx's *Critique of the Gotha Programme* (the passage so often referred to in which Marx drew the distinction between the two phases of communism), he must have noticed that Marx insists that even under the 'lower phase of communism' 'the producers do not exchange their produce' and that no class distinctions exist any longer 'because everybody is only a worker'. If the present Soviet system represents socialism then it follows that the distinction between the peasant and the worker should have become irrelevant and the member of the *kolkhoz* should be a worker *on a par* with the industrial producer. *Kolkhoz* trade and *kolkhoz* markets should then be relegated as anachronisms to a museum of antiquities. It is with such reasonings that Stalin deals in his article. A way out of the confusion would be to admit that the Soviet economy is still only a halfway-house between capitalism and socialism, not devoid even of features of pre-capitalist relations. But Stalinist orthodoxy cannot afford such an admission.

On a more theoretical level the problem is formulated as follows: does the law of value, in the Marxist sense, operate under socialism? In Marxist theory the 'law of value' is bound up exclusively and inseparably with the market economy in its pre-capitalist and capitalist varieties. The notion itself of value (i.e. exchange value as distinct from use value) does not exist outside production for the market, commodity exchange, and trade. By definition there is no room for it in a socialist economy, for under socialism the community is expected merely to distribute and allocate its social product—the members of the community are expected to produce for the common pool and to consume from the common pool, without exchanging their produce among themselves. There is no room for selling and buying or seller and buyer. In the Soviet Union a great deal of selling and buying is, of course, going on in various forms, including forms normally associated with a black market. The young Soviet economist remembers the fantastic inflation of prices on *kolkhoz* markets during the recent war and in the first post-war years. He remembers the depreciation of the rouble which compelled the government to carry out the drastic post-war currency reform. Marxist theory has explained to him money as the reflex or embodiment of pure value, springing into and fading out of existence together with the exchange of commodities. How then is the existence of money, not to speak of its irrational value movements, to be fitted into the picture of a socialist economy?

Stalin is trying to fit these phenomena into the theoretical picture. Since he must insist on the socialist character of the economy and at the same time on the Marxist orthodoxy of his views, he is compelled to produce an essay in squaring the circle. He tries to prove in terms of classical Marxist theory something which in those terms is an absurdity, namely that the law of value continues to operate under socialism. It is, of course, possible to hold such a view; and some socialist schools of thought have held it. But it is as little possible to argue it coherently in terms of Marx's theory as it would be to argue in terms of Copernican cosmology that the earth is flat.

II

Behind manufactured scholastic dogma loom serious practical problems. We have mentioned the new cadres of the economists and administrators whom Stalin addresses. This is how he himself sees those cadres:

'It might be said that all that has been stated here is correct and generally known but contains nothing new and that consequently there is no need to waste time on repetition of truisms. Of course, there is nothing new in all that, but it would be incorrect to think that it is not worth while to spend time on repeating some of the truths familiar to us. We, the leading nucleus, are joined every year by thousands of new young cadres, who burn with the desire to help us and to prove themselves but who do not have sufficient Marxist education and do not know many of the things familiar to us. . . . They are impressed and bewildered by the colossal achievements of Soviet power, they are made dizzy by the extraordinary successes of the Soviet régime, and they begin to imagine that Soviet power can "do anything". . . . Some comrades say that the party acted incorrectly when having seized power and nationalized the means of production in our country it preserved commodity production.'

It may well be that Stalin crudely exaggerates the

simple-mindedness of the 'young cadres' and thus sets up imaginary whipping-boys whom it is easy to belabour in controversy. It is difficult to believe that the 'young cadres' should be unaware of the experiment of war communism, which was nothing else but an abortive Bolshevik attempt to abolish the market economy. Whatever the truth, Stalin leaves no doubt that pressure for the abolition of market relationships has recently made itself felt in Soviet ruling groups. Since market relationships have had their main basis in the structure of farming, in its semi-private character, the pressure has actually been for a further radical transformation of farming and its absorption in the nationalized economy.

The present structure of the *kolkhoz* system is, as we have seen, characterized by an elaborate and unstable balance between private and collective interests. The private interest has tended to expand beyond prescribed limits; and the government has striven to impose and maintain the priority of the corporate interest. In this tug-of-war the balance has swayed now in one and now in the other direction. During the last war, when the so-called millionaire-*kolkhoznik* was the hero of the day, private interests obviously gained much scope. The post-war currency reform, confiscating the 'fortunes' made on *kolkhoz* markets, tilted the scales in favour of the collective interests. So did the recent merger of the *kolkhozy* into larger units. It is now clear that the merger had been decided upon after an acute controversy which had rent the last Politbureau since 1948–9. Apparently more extreme measures for the suppression of the private interest were advocated. Khrushchev, we know, proposed the formation of Agrotowns; and the abolition of the residual private farming carried on within the *kolkhozy* was also contemplated. It is now vaguely suggested that Voznessensky, the former head of *Gosplan* and member of the Politbureau, stood for even more extreme ('adventurist') policies designed not merely to restrict the private interest within the collective farms but to carry farming as a whole from collectivization to 'socialization'. It is impossible to say whether this was really so, because only one party to the controversy has been allowed to air its views; and as Stalin and his associates have sometimes in the past shown themselves quite capable of stealing clothes from their bathing adversaries, it may even be that the policies now adopted as those originally expounded by the excommunicated Voznessensky. Whatever the truth, after a moment of apparent hesitation over the more extreme measures, the ruling group has rejected them, holding that a *bouleversement* of farming would produce more economic and political disruption than the Soviet Union could at present afford.

Nevertheless, the problem of the market economy, or more specifically of *kolkhoz* trade, remains. The market economy, as Stalin points out, tends to come into conflict with the needs of central planning. It introduces a huge element of 'spontaneity' and unpredictability in a field which even without it would still remain relatively unpredictable. In the course of nearly a quarter of a century farming has eluded planning. Few of the targets set for the output of grain and for the breeding of livestock have been attained. That the contradiction between the elements of planning and those of a market economy constitute the greatest single cleavage within the Soviet economy no critically minded student could ever have doubted. Until recently Stalinist writers denied or explained away this contradiction. It is on it, however, that Stalin has now turned the limelight. In his letter to L. D. Yaroshenko he writes:

'It is therefore the task of the leading bodies to indicate in good time the growing contradictions and to take timely measures towards their overcoming. . . . This applies above all to such economic phenomena as the group property in collective farming and the circulation of commodities. Of course, at present we successfully utilize these for the development of the socialist economy. . . . They will undoubtedly be of benefit in the nearest future as well. But it would be unforgivable blindness not to see that at the same time these phenomena are already beginning to act as a brake on the powerful development of our productive forces, in so far as they hamper State planning in its striving to encompass the whole of the national economy, especially of the rural economy. There can be no doubt that the further we proceed the more will these phenomena act as a brake on the continued growth of our country's productive forces. Consequently, it is our task to liquidate these contradictions by way of a gradual transformation of *kolkhoz* property into national property and by way of a gradual substitution of the exchange of products for commodity circulation.'

It should be underlined that Stalin describes not merely the private interest of the *kolkhoznik* but even 'group ownership' of the *kolkhoz* as a brake on planning. He forecasts that the 'brake' is likely to act more powerfully in the future; and he sees the eventual solution in the complete assimilation of farming to socialized industry. If the present structure were to be left unchanged, he says, then the conflict between planning and market relationships would eventually assume critical forms. This diagnosis is undoubtedly realistic, and it would be a mistake to see in it a symptom of Soviet economic weakness. It is, on the contrary, only against the background of the stupendous growth of Soviet economic power in recent years that this diagnosis could be made and that the problem to which it points could arise.

Despite its enormous human and material *faux frais*, the Soviet planned economy has achieved a high degree of consolidation. Its basis and its volume have been growing with the continuous industrial revolution, with the expansion in productive capacities and in reserves of skilled manpower. Experience accumulated in a quarter of a century shows itself in improved techniques of planning. The firmer the foundations on which the

planned economy rests and the greater its dynamic ex-
pansiveness, the earlier, however, must it hit the limits
which market relationships impose on it, and the stronger
must be its tendency to eliminate anarchical 'spontaneity' from the whole system. This again is no matter of
abstract economic principle only. The practical issue at
stake is the adjustment of agriculture to industrial development. The supply of food to the rapidly growing
industrial population and the geographic redistribution
of food-producing centres to suit the changing industrial
map of the country have proved chronically inadequate.
These disproportions, if they were to persist, would slow
down or even bring to a standstill industrial expansion.
The stronger the Soviet economy is as a whole, especially
its industrial sector, the more does the present condition
of Soviet farming become a source of weakness.

This is the central issue behind Stalin's survey of the
Soviet economy. But here again dogmatic considerations
superimpose themselves on realistic analysis. What
Stalin has described is, in Marxist terms, a 'contradiction between productive forces and productive relationships', a contradiction inherent in all class society,
including any society which may be in transition from
capitalism to socialism. To the Marxist this contradiction is unthinkable under socialism. 'Productive relationships' mean nothing else than the property relations
prevailing in any given society and the corresponding
mutual connections between social classes and groups.
The 'contradiction between productive forces and productive relationships' is, in other words, the conflict
between the needs of economic development and established property relations. Under capitalism there is the
constant, latent or open, conflict between private property in means of production and the social interde-
pendence of the producers or, more generally, the social
character of the productive process. Only social ownership of means of production can, in the Marxist view,
resolve the conflict between productive forces and pro-

ductive relationships. In so far as private (or 'group')
ownership predominates over a vast sector of the Soviet
economy (farming) the conflict persists, albeit in new
form.

This conflict once again defies the accepted picture of
Soviet 'socialism'. Consequently, either that socialism is
exposed as a myth; or else it must be declared that the
contradiction between productive forces and relationships, far from being a characteristic of past society
only, remains a feature of socialism as well. In deference
to a canon of his own making, Stalin in fact argues that
this contradiction will be inherent in human society for
ever. One must assume that Stalin puts into these formulæ some other meaning which has little in common
with their accepted Marxist sense, for otherwise his
conclusion would be that under socialism and communism the needs of economic development would continue
to clash with the new forms of ownership, i.e. with
social ownership. In such a view the 'contradiction between productive forces and productive relationships'
would be transformed into an eternal, metaphysical
element of human history.

From Stalin's correspondence with the economists it
appears that this point of his argument has caused bewil-
derment even among people accustomed to accept every
word from his mouth with prescribed reverence. Marxism explains social revolutions as the violent processes
through which productive relationships are brought in
line with the development of productive forces. If
Stalin's argument were to be taken at its face value, it
might even imply the 'inevitability' of new revolutions
in Soviet society. This was the last thing he had intended
to suggest, as he hastens to explain in his letter to A. I.
Notkin. In his characteristic desire to invest every one of
his moves with the merits of an absolute socialist 'truth',
Stalin has simply projected a conflict which afflicts
present Soviet society on to the Marxist vision of fully
fledged socialism and communism. He has put his finger

on a current and potentially explosive issue and has hastened to add that the issue is not explosive at all, for in one form or another it is bound to reappear at every stage of human development.

III

Throughout his argument Stalin repeatedly puts his finger on some potentially explosive issue, then asserts that no issue can be explosive under the Soviet system and then again, forgetting this assertion, insists on the highly explosive nature of the issue in question. It would take us too far to go into all the scholastic twists and turns of his reasoning—only one or two illustrations will suffice.

The dichotomy between the planned sector of the economy and the market coincides broadly with the contradiction between town and country in the Soviet Union. Stalin begins with denying the mere fact of the contradiction. The country, he says, is no longer exploited by the town as it used to be under capitalism and therefore 'not a trace' has been left of their former antagonism. What has survived is a 'difference' between town and country, not a 'contradiction'.

The critic might be tempted to ask when a 'difference' becomes a 'contradiction'. The *kolkhoznik* sells food, the town-dweller buys it directly or through the medium of a State or co-operative trading organization. The seller aims at selling dearly, the buyer at buying cheaply. This remains so even if the State, which acts as the middle-man, pays the peasant low prices and charges the town-dweller high prices for food. The 'difference' between the rural seller and the urban buyer is obviously a 'contradiction'. The 'difference' between national ownership and State planning (prevalent in town) and 'group' and private ownership and market relations (prevalent in the country) is surely also a 'contradiction'—otherwise group ownership and market relationships would not impede planning. The distinction between 'differences' and 'contradictions' is merely a formula of bureaucratic scholasticism designed to conceal the gulf between the various sections of Soviet society.

Eventually, however, Stalin is driven back to realities and then he reveals that gulf once again. When some of his correspondents suggest to him that it might be advisable to transfer the Machine Tractor Stations from State ownership to collective farm ownership he argues against this proposal strongly and in part very convincingly. He puts forward two arguments. He points out, first, that the technical equipment of farming (tractors and heavy machines) must be constantly renewed if agriculture is to keep pace with the industrial revolution. The collective farms, he goes on, would not be in a position to finance their own re-equipment:

'What does it mean to withdraw hundreds of thousands of wheeled tractors and to replace them by caterpillar tractors, to replace tens of thousands of obsolescent combines and to produce new machines, say, for technical cultures? This involves expenses running into milliards which could return only over six to eight years. Only the State can take upon itself such expenditure, because it and it alone is in a position to bear the losses resulting from the withdrawal and replacement of obsolescent machinery, because it and it alone is in a position to bear such losses over six to eight years in expectation of eventual returns.'

We are thus told that the collective farms are not in a position to undertake medium-term investment necessary for the periodical modernization of their equipment. This is a somewhat specious argument, because the financial capacity of the *kolkhozy* depends largely on the government's price- and credit-policies. Stalin perhaps intended to say that the *kolkhozy* could not be relied upon to make the investments rather than to claim that they were economically absolutely in no position to make them. More relevant than this is, however, Stalin's second argument:

'Let us suppose for a moment that we have adopted comrades Sanina's and Venzher's proposals and have begun to sell . . . Machine Tractor Stations to the *kolkhozy*. What would be the consequence?

'In the first instance the *kolkhozy* would become owners of essential means of production. They would thus find themselves in an exceptional position such as no business concern in our country enjoys, for, as is well known, even our nationalized business concerns are not the owners of their means of production. How could this exceptional situation of the *kolkhozy* be justified, by what consideration of progress and advance? Could it be said that this situation would be conducive to raising *kolkhoz* property to the level of national property, that it would speed up the transition of our society from socialism to communism? Would it not be more correct to say that this would only lengthen the distance between *kolkhoz* property and national property and that it would not bring [our economy] closer to communism, but, on the contrary, take it further away from communism?

'The result would, secondly, be that the sphere of commodity circulation would be widened, because a colossal number of the means of agricultural production would find itself within the orbit of commodity circulation.'

In other words, if the allegedly socialist *kolkhozy* were to own the Machine Tractor Stations, the result would be an enormous strengthening of the anti-socialist elements in the Soviet economy. In this Stalin is undoubtedly right. *En passant* he reveals, however, that after more than two decades of collectivization Soviet policy *vis-à-vis* the peasantry is still saddled with the old dilemma: an impoverished peasantry does not produce enough food and raw materials for the town; but a peasantry enjoying material incentives which ensure high production accumulates more property than is safe for the régime and imparts to the market economy more momentum than is safe for the planned sector of the economy. Between the lines of Stalin's argument there lurks the fear of the *kulak-kolkhoz*. The idea of the transfer of Machine Tractor Stations to collective farms is probably more than the brainwave of a few economists. It is only natural that the wealthier *kolkhozy* should cast covetous glances on the Machine Tractor Stations. The acquisition of those Stations by them might indeed mark the beginning of a powerful development of modern capitalism in Russian farming. Alas, Stalin has not told his correspondents whether he is afraid here of a contradiction or of a mere difference between town and country; but he has left them in no doubt that the party will continue to stand, with all its might, between the collective farms and the Machine Tractor Stations.

IV

Stalin's recent writings offer a glimpse of the movement of ideas going on in the Soviet ruling circles behind the half-real and half-deceptive façade of uniformity. It is this movement that distinguishes present-day Russia from the Russia of the late 'thirties which was from head to foot stunned and petrified after the shock of the great purges. The movement of ideas reflects conflicting social aspirations and pressures which even a monolithic régime is not in a position to eliminate for good. Despite the rigid orthodox terms in which ideas are formulated, the present discussions are in some respects well ahead of earlier controversies within the Bolshevik Party, because they centre on issues which have arisen on a much higher level of economic development. New questions demand new answers, and Stalinism is vitally interested in finding these, even if orthodoxy compels it to look for the answers by roundabout ways and to formulate them in circumlocution and 'double-talk'.

The 'transition from socialism to communism' is at present the chief 'double-talk' formula for the discussion of real problems. All views are framed in its terms.

Since the formula refers to a future and hypothetical state of society, it sanctions up to a point exploration and experimental thinking, which were almost totally absent from an earlier phase of Stalinism. To the student of Soviet affairs who has followed over the years the violent campaigns against *uravnilovka* (egalitarianism) it is fascinating to watch how in the course of the arguments about the 'transition' some economists draw cautiously, timidly yet quite distinctly the vistas of a society which will no longer be afflicted by the economic inequality now prevailing in the Soviet Union. Ideas and notions which were banished as heresies not so long ago seem to creep back into visions of the future and there to experience a quasi-rehabilitation. The guesses about the future sometimes sound like reflections on the present—this is not the first time that Utopia is either an implied critique of existing society or an escape from it. Things being in Russia what they are, authority's sudden and angry reactions against flights of experimental thought are inevitable. Yet this particular dream, the dream about the higher phase of communism, has been officially licensed and encouraged; and the Soviet citizen has even sometimes been led to believe that the 'transition' is not a matter for his 'children and grandchildren' but something which his own generation can and must achieve.

There is something profoundly paradoxical in all this. The present rulers of the Soviet Union require on the one hand the Soviet citizen to show a blind faith in, and a pious devotion to, Soviet institutions and policies *such as they are*. In this respect the Soviet rulers are more conservative than even the most conservative governments, for none require from their citizens quite as much faith in and enthusiasm for the established order. On the other hand, Stalinism also instils in the Soviet people the revolutionary conviction that most of these exalted institutions and policies deserve to be scrapped or radically changed in the transition from socialism to communism. Thus Stalinism works to impose a standstill upon the minds and the thoughts of the people and at the same time it desires to keep those thoughts and minds on the move, searching for new worlds.

Stalin has now sounded a note of caution. He has warned the 'young cadres', lured by the 'higher phase', that the transition from socialism to communism is a long uphill road. Years ago he used to scold those who spoke about 'objective laws' setting limits to governmental action. 'There are no fortresses which the Bolsheviks cannot seize' was his slogan then. Now he scolds those who ignore the 'objective laws' of a socialist economy or aspire to modify them. His insistence on the validity of economic laws under socialism has, for all its turgid scholasticism, symptomatic significance. When Stalin speaks so emphatically about the objective laws and warns against 'economic adventurers', he surely applies the brake to economic policy. His invocation of the economic laws is his substitute for the cry: Moderation! Moderation!

'With us,' Stalin, says, 'commodity production and trade are as necessary at present as they were, say, thirty years ago.' Thirty years ago N.E.P. had just been introduced; farming was broken up into twenty-odd million farms; and some industries were just being transferred to capitalist ownership. Stalin's obvious overstatement serves an 'educational' purpose. It amounts to a warning against over-hasty experiments with farming and the market economy. *En passant* Stalin has made the startling revelation that 'some comrades'—is it Voznessensky again?—have advocated the complete nationalization of all farming. Stalin agrees that national or social ownership of the whole economy, including farming, is the pre-condition for communism which will know no market economy and no money. But he gives to understand that this will be a protracted process to be completed perhaps only in that remote future when capitalism will have vanished in most countries and even the State will have withered away. He explores two methods for the solution of the problems of farming and of the market economy. He rejects direct absorption of farming by the State on grounds of political and social impracticability; and he foreshadows the gradual extension of planning by a single authority to both sectors of the economy and also to the distribution of farm produce.

In his article, dated 1 February 1952, Stalin did not go beyond this general conclusion. He did not specify how he envisaged the gradual extension of planning to collective farming and to the distribution of farm produce. In the letter to Sanina and Venzher dated eight months later (28 September 1952), he offers a more specific plan. The collective farmer, he argues, cannot be brought to accept social ownership as long as he finds trade in farm produce profitable. The government cannot 'abolish' trade, but it must offer to the peasantry something more profitable than trade, namely the direct exchange of industrial goods for farm produce, the exchange of products (*produkto-obmen*) instead of the exchange of commodities. A modest beginning has been made with farms specializing in the cultivation of technical plants. The government buys up their entire crops and pays them partly in money and partly in industrial goods. This practice should be gradually extended to other farms and money should gradually be eliminated from the transactions. Stalin points to the limiting factor which does not allow for a large-scale extension of the practice in the near future: the government is not in a position to offer the collective farmers industrial goods in quantities and assortments which would induce them to give up trade. The key to the solution is to be found in the town, not in the countryside; but the town has not yet produced it. 'Such a system', Stalin writes, 'requires an enormous increase in the output of goods which the town supplies to the country and therefore we shall have to introduce it without especial haste, only as urban output grows. But introduce it we must, unflaggingly, without wavering, step by step, thus reducing the sphere of commodity circulation. . . .'

As is usual with Stalin, the seriousness of what he has to say grows as he leaves theory and dogma for practical policy. What he foreshadows here may well prove the most significant economic reform contemplated in the Soviet Union since the collectivization of farming. In a nutshell these passages may be said to contain a broad plan for the gradual elimination of the market economy. Unlike collectivization, the reform is envisaged as an evolutionary process, the tempo of which will be dictated by the pace of further industrialization and the extent to which the growth of the Soviet national income may allow the government simultaneously to participate in the armaments race, to go on with massive investment in heavy industry, and to increase rapidly the output of consumer goods especially for rural consumption. Its multiple economic and political commitments may yet force the government to postpone the reform to an indefinite future. But even in the most favourable circumstances, a reform of this kind would require a decade or two for its successful completion. A great abundance of industrial consumer goods is only the first condition of its success. There still remain the imponderables, the mental habits, the social customs, and the economic 'prejudices' of the peasantry which have all to be overcome before the *kolkhoznik* gives up the *kolkhoz* market for *produkto-obmen*. Although it has proved possible to drive the *muzhik* into the collective farm and to compel and induce him to stay in it, it has so far proved impossible to drive out of him his attachment to property, as Stalin now implicitly admits. The peasant's individualism has been kept within bounds and subdued but not destroyed. In a poverty-stricken nation, amid the miseries of the first decades of collectivization, it has still been property and trade that have offered or promised the peasant relative well-being and security. Not before planned economy can offer him much greater well-being and security can it begin to undo the rural market. Stalin's cautious approach to this problem seems therefore well justified.

The note of caution rings even more broadly in Stalin's 'three conditions' for the transition to communism. In Stalin's own words—'in order to *prepare* the *transition* to communism in reality and not merely in declarations it is necessary to fulfil *at least* three essential *preliminary* conditions' (My italics). This sounds quite differently from the glib assurances that Soviet society is already in the process of that transition. The 'three conditions' include: (1) the continued intensive development of the country's industrial resources; (2) the slow and gradual adjustment of collective farming to the nationalized sector of the economy and the gradual abolition of trade;[1] and (3) the raising of the standards of living and of the cultural standards, the reduction of the working day '*at least*' to six or rather to five hours, the doubling (again '*at least*') of real wages, and the spread of education which would allow the contradiction between brain work and manual labour to be abolished. As this statement appeared on the eve of the Nineteenth Congress of the party, it led commentators to expect an imminent shortening of the working day, which at eight hours is still longer than it was in the 1930's. The Congress, however, has not reduced working hours, which also indicates that Stalin's 'three conditions' are regarded as a long-term programme.

Stalin had intended to give the 'young cadres' the measure of the great distance which separates Soviet society from communism and to indicate in what way that distance might be shortened. What he has actually indicated is, in Marxist terms, the distance which still separates the Soviet Union not from communism but from socialism.

---

[1] 'It is necessary, secondly, by way of *gradual transitions*, effected with benefit to the collective farms and consequently to the whole of society, to raise collective property to the level of national property and to replace commodity circulation by the system of *produkto-obmen*, also by way of *gradual transitions*, so that the central government or some other social-economic directing body should be able to encompass the whole output of social production in the interest of society.'

PART FOUR

RUSSIA IN TRANSITION

THE BERIA AFFAIR[1]

BERIA'S downfall, announced on 10 July 1953, marks the end of a distinct phase in Russia's political evolution after Stalin. During that phase which lasted from March till the end of June the advocates of reform at home and conciliation abroad were in the ascendant, while the die-hards of Stalinism and the 'anti-appeasers' were compelled to yield one position after another.

The East German revolt of 16 and 17 June 1953 brought into play a new factor which threw back the reformers and conciliators and allowed their opponents to strike a counter-blow, the first since Stalin's death. A coalition of the most diverse groups, interests, and motives came to the fore with the battle cry: Enough of 'liberalism'! Enough of appeasement! Enough of the betrayal of Stalinist orthodoxy! To the world's amazement, Beria, Stalin's countryman, henchman, admiring biographer, and for many years chief policeman, was denounced as the arch-traducer of Stalinism.

The Beria affair is undoubtedly an incident in the personal rivalry between Stalin's successors. It represents one stage in the process by which a candidate for the vacant post of the autocrat may strive to eliminate his competitors. But personal rivalry is only one of the elements of the drama: and in itself it is of secondary importance. More significant is the conflict of principles and policies hidden behind the clash of personalities— the world is interested in the policies rather than the personalities which are going to emerge victorious.

[1] This essay was written in July 1953 as a Postscript to *After Stalin*.

Let us briefly survey the trend of Soviet policies since Stalin's death in order to see which are the major issues at stake.

From March till the middle of June 1953, one domestic reform followed upon another in close succession. The Stalin cult was virtually abolished. A campaign of 'enlightenment' was in progress, designed to make it impossible to replace that cult by the adulation of any other Leader. The administration was being overhauled and shaken from its Byzantine totalitarian rigidity. A fairly comprehensive amnesty was decreed. The frame-up of the Kremlin doctors was declared null and void. The inquisitorial methods of the political police were bluntly condemned. The rule of law was proclaimed. Strong emphasis was placed on the constitutional rights of the citizen. Newspapers asked almost openly for the abolition of censorship and official control. (*The Literary Gazette*, for instance, frankly demanded that the Soviet theatre be allowed to manage its own affairs without outside interference, a demand which nobody would have dared to raise during the Stalin era and which obviously set an infectious example to others.) The need for the 'monolithic' outlook was implicitly or even explicitly questioned at almost every step. Free expression of views was encouraged; and the holder of unorthodox views was no longer labelled an enemy, a traitor, or a foreign agent. High officials were demoted merely on the ground that they abused their power and acted unconstitutionally; no predatory or counter-revolutionary intent was attributed to them. The relaxation of the over-centralistic method of government was noticeable above all in the dismissal of Russifiers from high office in the Ukraine, in Georgia, and other outlying Union Republics. Russification was emphatically disavowed. Together with the cessation of anti-Semitic incitement, these moves promised a new and hopeful beginning in the treatment of the smaller nationalities.

Last but not least, the government ordered a revision

of the targets of the current economic plans. Consumer industries were to raise their output. A higher standard of living and contentment of the masses were obviously regarded as vital preconditions for the success of the new policy.

A new spirit made itself felt in the conduct of foreign affairs. Moscow consistently exercised its influence in favour of a truce in Korea; and not even Syngman Rhee's provocations diverted the Russians (or the Chinese or the North Koreans) from this path. In Europe, Malenkov's government began 'to explore the lines of retreat from Germany'.[1]

It is enough to recall here the moves made by Soviet diplomacy only during the week which preceded the Berlin revolts:

After General Chuikov had been recalled from Berlin the whole policy of the Pieck-Ulbricht government was dramatically reversed. The 'iron curtain' between Eastern and Western Germany was nearly demolished. Labour policy was reversed. The struggle between the government and the Evangelical Church was called off; and the Church regained its former privileges. Collectivization of farming was stopped. The farmers who had fled to Western Germany were invited to come back and take possession of their property. Private capital was also invited to return to industry and trade.

From the Russian viewpoint these moves made no sense at all unless they were part and parcel of a policy calculated to bring about the unification of Germany and the withdrawal of occupation armies. There was little doubt in Berlin that Moscow was really prepared to abandon the government of Pieck and Ulbricht. So strongly indeed did Soviet representatives in Berlin encourage this belief and so frankly did they negotiate with non-communist leaders about a change of régime that by this alone the Russians themselves unwittingly induced the people of Berlin to descend upon the streets,

[1] *Russia After Stalin.*

to clamour for the resignation of the communist government, and to storm that government's offices. 'Russia is willing to abandon her puppets—let us remove them at once!' this was the idea behind the German revolt.

In the same week, on 10 June, Moscow established diplomatic relations with Austria and proclaimed an end to the régime of occupation there. Restrictions on interzonal traffic were abolished in Austria as well. And on the same day, as a side-line, Moscow solemnly renounced all its claims on Turkey, the claims that played so fatal a role in the opening phases of the cold war.

What was surprising in all these developments, domestic and foreign, was their extraordinary consistency and apparently frictionless progress. Stalin's successors showed no sign of hesitation in pursuing the new course. They betrayed no second thoughts. They seemed to bask in the glory of unaccustomed generosity.

Was it possible, one wondered, that the die-hards of Stalinism and other opponents of 'appeasement' should be so weak and discredited that they should not be able to put a brake upon the new course? Or were they perhaps retreating tactically and merely waiting until the new policy had run into serious trouble?

* * *

Where did Beria stand in all this? To which faction did he belong?

In watching the Russian scene it is not difficult to arrive, by processes of deduction and analysis, at a definition of the broad viewpoints and political conceptions contending for acceptance by the ruling group. Nor is it very difficult to see the sectional interests and aspirations reflected in the competing conceptions. The broad forces aligned with or arrayed against one another throw their shadows sharply enough even across the veil of secrecy that surrounds them for the outsider to be able to guess the approximate disposition of those forces. But only in exceptional cases is it possible to venture even a guess about the attitude of this or that official personality on any specific issue.

In *Russia After Stalin* the supposition was expressed that 'in the inner councils of the party Beria did not necessarily represent the anti-liberal attitude of the police', that he may, on the contrary, have acted against the 'die-hards of the police' as one of the promoters of reform.

This supposition appears to have in the meantime been borne out by the facts. In the last period of his activity Beria represented the curious paradox of a semi-liberal police chief in a totalitarian State. The period up to the East German revolt might indeed be described as Beria's hundred days.

Beria took upon himself the responsibility for two major political acts, two unforgivable 'crimes' in the eyes of the die-hards of Stalinism and their associates. First, he humiliated the political police when he exposed its practices in connection with the 'doctors' plot'. Next, he offended 'Great Russian chauvinism' when he, the Georgian, called for an end to Russification in Georgia, in the Ukraine, in the Baltic lands, and in Central Asia.

Both these acts, the former more explicitly than the latter, had ostensibly been endorsed by the other party leaders. But as Minister of the Interior Beria was identified with these acts more closely than anybody else. No wonder that some of the old hands of the political police, resentfully straining to recover their sacred right to extort 'confessions' from their victims, and the Great Russian chauvinists, joined hands to wreak vengeance on him.

Beria was less directly associated with the conduct of foreign affairs; but, as a member of the Politbureau (now the Presidium), he exercised a strong influence in that field, too. Bolshevik foreign policy has never been made by the Foreign Minister of the day, Molotov, Vishinsky, Litvinov, or Chicherin—it has always been the prerogative of the Politbureau. That foreign and domestic policies are closely interdependent has been an axiom. The man in charge of domestic security must therefore have had a considerable say in foreign affairs as well. Beria certainly had a decisive say in the affairs of Eastern Germany and generally of Eastern Europe, which had a direct bearing on Russia's internal security, on the one hand, and on diplomacy, on the other. Thus his opponents could easily blame him for 'appeasement' as well as for the domestic reforms.

From March to June Beria acted in close alliance with Malenkov. Together they swayed the Presidium, probably against Molotov's and certainly against Khrushchev's opposition or semi-opposition. Jointly they represented the strongest block of power within the Presidium. The new policy aroused great hopes and was undoubtedly very popular; and as long as this was so, nobody could challenge Malenkov's and Beria's joint authority.

(Against this interpretation the old argument may be advanced that under a totalitarian régime the states of the popular mind and the social, cultural, and moral trends at work in society are of no political importance. In his criticism of *Russia After Stalin*, Mr. George F. Kennan, for instance, writes that the 'majority of students of modern totalitarianism . . . feel that *if the ruling group remains united, vigilant* and ruthless, it need not defer extensively to, or be seriously influenced by, subjective feelings within the populace at large.' And again: 'In general, totalitarian leaders *who retain their internal unity* and their ruthlessness can scoff at subjective states of the popular mind. . . .'[1]

Mr. Kennan's words, written before Beria's fall, reflected an assumption that there was no need for Western policy to take into account any genuine divisions within the Soviet ruling group, because no such divisions existed. This assumption has been proved wrong. But what conclusion is to be drawn from the fact that the Soviet ruling group does not 'remain united' and does

[1] My italics.

not 'retain its internal unity'? Then surely the 'subjective states of the popular mind' do acquire some political significance? And those states of mind may in part even account for the differences within the ruling group itself?)

From the beginning, however, the forces opposed to the Malenkov-Beria policy were formidable. The old hands of the political police were not idle. Some party stalwarts were shocked by the all round break with the old-established canons of Stalinism. Some chiefs of armed forces pondered with alarm the implications of the quasi-liberal reforms: would the reforms not cause a slump in labour discipline and imperil the armament programmes? By dint of tradition the army has been the mouthpiece of 'Great Russian chauvinism' and has viewed with suspicion and hostility the 'centrifugal' nationalisms of the outlying Republics. Some marshals and generals could not adopt a favourable attitude towards a foreign policy obviously directed towards an eventual withdrawal of the occupation armies from Germany and Austria.

But the coalition of shocked Stalinist die-hards, resentful policemen, and anxious generals was helpless as long as the new policy was triumphantly carried forward on a tide of popular enthusiasm. The first hitches apparently occurred on the home front. To judge from circumstantial evidence, labour discipline did slump in industry; and collective farms lagged with food deliveries. But these hitches were either not serious enough to permit the opponents of the new policy to launch a frontal attack on it, or else they did not provide convenient ground for such an attack.

It was Eastern Germany that gave the opponents of the new policy the opportunity they had eagerly awaited.

The Germans who on 16 and 17 June descended upon the streets, clamouring for the dismissal of the government of Pieck and Ulbricht, assailing the People's Police, and meeting Russian tanks with a hail of stones did in fact bring about an upheaval; but the upheaval took place in Moscow, not in Berlin.

Almost certainly a cry against 'appeasement' went up at once within the walls of the Kremlin. Army chiefs could now argue that it was the army that had to bear the consequences of the neck-breaking political experiments started by the civilians; that order reigned in Eastern Germany as long as General Chuikov ruled there with an iron hand; that the trouble began as soon as the general had been replaced by Semyonov, as High Commissioner, and a civilian régime had been established; and that then it was the army that had to rescue that régime.

Starting from the German issue the critics could turn against the new policy as a whole. They could point out that not only Germany but the West at large was receiving Russian concessions as proof of Russian weakness; and that Washington in particular was using these concessions as the starting-point for an intensified onslaught on Russia's positions in Eastern and Central Europe.

Moreover, the ruling group saw that the new policy was indeed becoming a source of weakness for Russia: it plunged the whole of Eastern Europe into a turmoil; it caused a rapid deterioration in Russia's bargaining position; and it threatened to rob Russia of the fruits of her victory in the Second World War, without any compensating gains.

The 'appeasers' may still have argued that the new line had not yet been given a chance; that it would be wrong to abandon it immediately after it had encountered the first difficulties; and that only by persisting patiently in the policy of concessions could the Soviet government reap its benefits.

But after the earthquake in Eastern Germany, after the tremors in Hungary and Czechoslovakia, after all the calls for a tough policy which resounded from Washington, the argument against 'appeasement' carried more weight in the Kremlin.

In Russia as in the United States there exist groups which hold the view that all peace-seeking is futile; these groups view with *Schadenfreude* any setback suffered by the conciliators. The position of such groups was now greatly enhanced: the advocates of a tough policy in the West had effectively played into their hands.

There is no reason, however, to assume that after 16 and 17 June these extremists became the real masters of Soviet policy. The core of the ruling group still consists of men prepared to seek agreement with the West. But even the men 'of the centre' must have been affected by the arguments against 'appeasement'. They had to admit that the conduct of Soviet policy since Stalin's death was rather inept in some respects.

They had to admit that Moscow was over-hasty in making concessions and over-zealous in demonstrating its willingness to make further and more far-reaching concessions. Official spokesmen had many times confidently stated that the government would never accept Washington's demand that Russia must yield substantial ground before the West opened negotiations. In fact Malenkov's government behaved as if it had tacitly accepted that demand: it did make concessions in advance of negotiations.

Even from the viewpoint of the Soviet appeaser the initiation of the mild course in Eastern Germany turned out to have been 'premature'. It provoked a near collapse of the communist régime there. From the Soviet viewpoint it would have been justifiable to take such risks only after the West had agreed to an all round withdrawal of the occupation armies. The undoing of the communist régime in Eastern Germany would then be the price Russia paid for a German settlement and a stop to the armament race. But to have paid this price so early in the game was the peak of folly from the Kremlin's viewpoint.

Thus even the men of the 'centre' who had hitherto

backed the new policy had to recognize the need for a change in tone and perhaps in tactics, even if they were not at all inclined to give up the quest for 'peaceful co-existence'. Finding themselves under deadly fire from the extreme groups, they were all too anxious to disclaim responsibility for the 'appeasement' of recent months, and to throw the blame for it on someone else.

The East German revolt also provided an opening for an attack on domestic reform. To be sure, not all the adherents of conciliation abroad stood also for reform at home; and not all the reformers need have been appeasers. Nevertheless there exists a broad correspondence between the two aspects of policy; and amid the tension created by the events in Germany both aspects became vulnerable.

The sense of security and the optimism which had characterized Russia's mood in the spring had gone. The cry for vigilance resounded anew and with fresh vigour. Soldier, policeman, and Stalinist stalwart could point accusing fingers at the advocates of reform: Your policy, so they could say, has already brought disaster in Berlin and caused dangerous trouble in Budapest and Prague. Soon it may bring disaster nearer home. In Moscow the people are already whispering about an impending depreciation of the rouble, and the Minister of Finance was compelled to speak about this in public. Discipline is becoming slack in the factories. Trouble is brewing in the collective farms. The newspapers in their new-fangled zeal for free criticism are sapping popular respect for authority. If you are allowed to continue this policy, you will bring about a 16 June here in Moscow!

The phantom of a 16 June in Moscow struck fear into the hearts of the reformers and paralysed their wills.

* * *

In *Russia After Stalin* three possible variants of development were discussed: (*a*) democratic regeneration; (*b*) a relapse into Stalinism; and (*c*) a military dictatorship. It was pointed out that the prerequisite for a military dictatorship would be a war-like threat to Russia from the West.

The picture of events is in fact more confused and contradictory than the theoretical forecast. *Grau ist jede Theorie, und ewig grün ist des Lebens Baum.* Yet the theoretical analysis still provides the clue to the picture.

The East German events, followed by the call to revolt addressed to Eastern Europe from the West, presented Moscow with a substitute for a 'war-like threat', with half such a threat. This was not enough to bring about a military coup. But it was quite enough to bring back into action that coalition of groups in army and police which had shown its hand in the affair of the Kremlin doctors in January. Roughly the same combination of cliques which had concocted the doctors' plot carried out a semi-coup against the reformers and 'appeasers' after 16 and 17 June.

Under this attack the alliance between Malenkov and Beria broke down. The attack was evidently powerful enough to make Malenkov feel that he could save his own position only by shifting his ground and throwing Beria to the lions. And Malenkov succeeded indeed in saving his position.

'The die-hards of the security police may still try to rally and fight to save their skins. [These words were written in April 1953.] They may fight back from the provinces and they may try to regain the ground lost in Moscow. They may have influential associates and accomplices inside the Kremlin. They may try to remove Malenkov and his associates, denouncing them as apostates, secret Trotskyite-Bukharinites, and imperialist agents, and presenting themselves as Stalin's only true and orthodox heirs.' (*Russia After Stalin.*)

This has come true, only that so far Beria, not Malenkov, has been 'removed' and 'denounced as apostate'; and Malenkov has sought to insure his position by consenting to play the part of Beria's chief denouncer.

Beria was in a peculiarly vulnerable position. His name had been associated with the darkest aspects of Stalinism in the last fifteen years, with concentration camps, mass deportations and thought control, with the iron curtain, and with the purge trials in the satellite countries. He had performed all the unsavoury jobs assigned to him by Stalin. Yet after his master's death he unmasked himself as a *dvurushnik*, and a 'liberal' at heart. His own police despised him as a 'liberal'; and the people hated him as the chief of the police. His head, the head which belonged to the 'most powerful and most dreaded man of Russia', was therefore the easiest prize to win for the opponents of reform. Both the police and the people almost certainly rejoiced at his downfall. The people believed that only now would the era of freedom begin for good, while the die-hards of the political police were confident that only now did the crazy spring of liberal reform come to an end.

On the face of it the fall of Beria might be seen as a necessary stage in Russia's democratic evolution; and thus Malenkov has vaguely presented it. The chief accusation he levelled against Beria was that Beria had conspired to place the political police above party and government and thus to block the road of reform. Beria, so Malenkov stated, carried out the recent reforms only because he had to: these reforms having been decided on the joint initiative of the Central Committee and the Presidium, Beria pretended to carry them out loyally, while in fact he obstructed their execution. As if to confirm this version, the Central Committee restated its criticism of the Stalin cult, its opposition to the adulation of any Leader, and its determination to secure 'collective leadership', free debate, and the rule of law.

If this were all one might indeed see the downfall of Beria as a further stage in Russia's revulsion against Stalinism. But this is not all.

What is ominous in this grim affair is, of course, not Beria's downfall but the manner in which it was brought

about. He was denounced as traitor and enemy of the
party and the people, and as an agent of foreign imperialism who aimed at the restoration of capitalism. This is
the 'classical amalgam' of the Stalinist purges of the
1930's. Thus, the re-enactment of the Witches' Sabbath,
which failed to come off in January, appears to have
begun after all, with Beria, instead of the Kremlin
doctors, hovering 'through the fog and filthy air'.

The reproduction of the 'amalgam' of the 1930's
makes a mockery of the claim of the ruling group that it
defended the principle of collective leadership against
Beria. That principle implies unhampered expression of
political differences within the leading group and ultimately within the party as a whole. But who will dare to
speak his mind freely when he has reason to fear that
for this he may be denounced as traitor and foreign
agent? The Stalinist amalgam rules out free discussion
and consequently 'collective leadership'.

If it was possible to see a promise of democratic
regeneration in Russia after Stalin's death, this was so
because denunciations of this sort had disappeared—
they were becoming rarer and rarer even during Stalin's
last years. The many high officials demoted between
March and June were not labelled foreign agents, spies,
or adherents of capitalism. They were charged with
concocting false accusations, abusing power, imposing
policies of Russification, and so on. These were plausible
charges, self-explanatory within a certain political context, and fitting in with the circumstances in which the
dismissed men, whether guilty or not, had operated. The
charges were made in a moderate and sober language in
which there was no hint of a witch hunt.

In contrast to this the accusations levelled against
Beria were full of irrational, demonological overtones;
and the world was asked to believe that the man who was
in charge of Russia's domestic security during the
Second World War was an agent of foreign imperialism.

The meaning of the Beria affair emerges even more

conclusively from the fact that his fall became the signal for a new drive against the 'nationalisms' of the Georgians, Ukrainians, and other non-Russian nationalities. It was no sheer coincidence that during the 'liberal spring' Great Russian chauvinism was kept in check and the need was proclaimed to give more scope to the aspirations and demands of the non-Russian Republics.

Policy towards the smaller nations is the most sensitive barometer of the general atmosphere of the Soviet Union. Liberalization means less central control and more autonomy for non-Russians. Police rule implies strict centralization; and its tightening usually leads to a drive against the 'bourgeois' nationalisms of the outlying Republics.

Between March and June the talk was, characteristically, against operating the bogy of '*alleged* bourgeois nationalism' in the non-Russian provinces. In what seemed a long overdue act of historical justice the Russifiers were dismissed from office in Tiflis and Kiev. It should perhaps be recalled that the Stalin era began precisely with a struggle against the 'nationalist deviationists' in Georgia and the Ukraine. It was on this subject that Lenin, mortally ill, wrote his last, great, angry, and stirring letter to the party. (The author has read the full text of this letter which has remained unpublished till this day.) In it Lenin expressed his sense of shame and even of personal guilt which Stalin's drive against the nationalist deviationists had aroused in him. He warned the party against the Great Russian chauvinism of the Soviet bureaucracy and of Stalin in particular, against the barbarous violence of that 'truly Russian Great Bully', who, evoking the need for strict central government, would oppress, insult, and humiliate the non-Russian nationalities. Lenin passionately argued that it would be a thousand times better for the Soviet Republic even to forgo the advantages of centralized government than 'to deliver the smaller nationalities into the hands of the Great Russian Bully'.

There was therefore a curious historical symmetry in the circumstance that immediately after Stalin's death the Georgian and Ukrainian issues reappeared on the agenda and that this time an attempt was made to tame the 'truly Russian Great Bully'.

But 'the Great Bully' seems to have come back to bait the 'bourgeois' nationalists of Georgia and the Ukraine; and his return is the surest sign of some reaction against the progressive reforms of preceding months.

* * *

The struggle is still on, however, and its outcome has hardly been decided. The die-hards of Stalinism have scored only half a victory.

In some respect the Beria affair is quite unique and cannot even be compared with any of Stalin's great purges.

None of Stalin's victims wielded on the eve of a purge power comparable to Beria's; and none had as much of a following within the bureaucracy. Stalin finally destroyed Bukharin, Zinoviev, Kamenev, and their like after having first patiently, slyly, and in the course of many years deprived them of the last shred of power, discredited them, and rendered them harmless. On the eve of his trial Tukhachevsky was powerful enough as a military personality; but he had no political standing. Yagoda was a mere executor of Stalin's will. In 1936–8 Stalin had already his hands firmly on all levers of power and nobody dared to challenge his autocratic position.

Not so Malenkov. He has apparently embarked upon the slippery road of purges even before he stands on his own feet. His leadership is not yet acknowledged. His position of power is not yet consolidated. He must still speak and act as one of a team. The party is 'rallying' not behind 'Comrade Malenkov' but 'around the Central Committee'. Malenkov's position today is not appreciably stronger than Beria's was yesterday.

If it was possible to overthrow Beria so easily what guarantee is there that Malenkov cannot be disgraced with just as little effort? If party meetings could be so rapidly persuaded to acclaim the fall of one triumvir, may they not look upon the destruction of any other triumvir with equal indifference?

The fate of Stalin's successors may yet prove less similar to that of Stalin than to that of Danton, Robespierre, Desmoulins, who sent each other to the guillotine, while none of them enjoyed exclusive authority, with the result that all were destroyed. It is, of course, also possible that after a series of purge trials one of Stalin's successors may finally emerge as the new autocrat; but this is by no means certain.

The divisions in the ruling group reflect in the last instance conflicting pressures exerted upon it by outside forces which in the long run work either towards a military dictatorship or towards democratic regeneration. The Beria affair represents therefore only one moment in the kaleidoscopic movement of contemporary Russian history.

The army chiefs no longer watch the scene in passivity and silence. Their influence was clearly discernible in the affair of the Kremlin doctors. It was even more distinct in the Beria affair. Without the army's assured support Malenkov would not have dared to strike at Beria, who nominally still had the whole body of the political police under his orders, and who, at any rate, could still rely on some section of the police to rally to his defence. It was no matter of chance that Moscow's Press and radio gave so much prominence to the speeches against Beria made by Marshals Zhukov, Vassilevsky, Sokolovsky, Govorov, and others. During the great Stalinist purges the leaders of the officers' corps did not so conspicuously appear on the political stage. Even so, Stalin felt his position to be threatened by Tukhachevsky. How much more may the position of Stalin's successors be imperilled by the marshals, whose military glory and popular appeal are far superior to Tukhachevsky's.

'Malenkov's government has struck a blow at the

political police. [This quotation is also from *Russia After Stalin*.] If effective the blow must cause a shift in the whole structure of the régime. One of its two props has been weakened, perhaps shattered. On the face of it, this upsets the equilibrium of the régime and tends to increase the importance of the other prop—the army. If the party has deprived itself of the ability to oppose the political police to the army, the army may become the decisive factor in domestic affairs.'

Paradoxically, the régime now seems to make an attempt to repair that shattered prop, the political police, with the army's help. But for some time to come, until the Beria faction is completely eliminated, the political police will remain in a state of disarray, robbed of its normal striking power; more than ever the government will have to rely for its internal security on the army. It must take some time before the structure of power characteristic of Stalinism is restored, if it can be restored at all. Until then a gap will yawn between the galvanized Stalinist method of government and the un-Stalinist mechanics of power. Across this gap a potential Bonaparte once again casts his shadow.

Nor have the forces vanished which drove the ruling group to decree the reforms of last spring, although at the moment they may have suffered a severe setback. The reforms could not have sprung merely from Beria's, or from anybody else's, whim and ambition; they met a need felt deeply and widely by the nation. Malenkov and his associates still pay a tribute to the popular mood when they go on declaring that they intend to pursue the course initiated after Stalin's death. The popular mood compels them to tread a twisted path rather cautiously, and it may even compel them to keep part of their promise. Moreover, the recent reforms corresponded to Russia's new social structure and outlook which, although formed during the Stalin era, have become incompatible with Stalinism.

No shift within the ruling group, no court intrigue, no

G

coup or counter-coup, and not even bloody purges can obliterate these basic factors, which continue to operate against the inertia of Stalinism. If they are not destroyed by a new world war and if they are not unduly cramped by fear of war, the popular mood and the urges of society will, sooner or later, force open the road of reform once again. And then they will keep it open more firmly than they did in the liberal spring of 1953.

A REPLY TO CRITICS[1]

MY book *Russia After Stalin*, which I wrote and concluded within a few weeks after Stalin's death, is appearing in a French translation shortly before the first anniversary of that event. This is a short interval; yet it has been crowded with startling events, and during it Russia has moved quite a distance from where she stood on 6 March 1953. It is enough to recall what some of the best known commentators and experts predicted at the time, to realize how far indeed Russia is now from that point of departure. Some of the experts, for instance, argued, not without superficial logic, that in a Police State the police was the decisive factor of power, and that consequently Beria, its head, was by definition Stalin's real successor, sure to oust Malenkov and Molotov. Other reputable analysts assured us stolidly that there was and could be 'nothing new in the East', because Stalin had settled beforehand the issue of the succession and because his heirs, tied by the strongest bonds of solidarity, saw eye to eye with one another over all major issues of policy.

The most obtuse Stalinists and the bitterest anti-communists expressed this view with equal self-confidence. Curiously enough, this was also the view held even later by so intelligent a writer as Mr. George Kennan and expressed in his critique of my book. I know of another very shrewd man, the Moscow Ambassador of a great Western power, who spent the whole evening of 9 July 1953 arguing that my analysis of the Russian situation, given in *Russia After Stalin*, was utterly

[1] This 'Reply' was originally written for the French monthly *Esprit* (March 1954).

wrong because it presupposed a cleavage within the Soviet ruling group. He, the Ambassador, knew from close observation and long study that no such cleavage existed: that Malenkov, Beria, Molotov, and Khrushchev thought and acted in unison, knowing full well that their chances of survival depended on their absolute unity. Having thus destroyed my analysis and hypothesis once for all, His Excellency went to bed only to awaken next morning to the dramatic news about Beria's downfall. . . .

I know well where my own work might gain from some corrections, and what revision would be advisable in the light of recent events. But such corrections and revisions would not yet go beyond retouching a paragraph here and changing slightly the emphasis of my argument there. Far from refuting my prognostication, events have confirmed it; and they have done so in the only way in which they confirm a theoretical formula, namely by showing a pattern of development which, although it harmonizes basically with the prediction, is naturally more complicated and dynamic than any theoretical formula.

My prognostication has not been basically refuted by events perhaps because from the outset I approached my task somewhat more modestly than many another writer on this subject. I did not pretend to know what would be the fate of this or that personality in the Soviet ruling group. I drew no personal horoscope for Malenkov, or Beria, or Khrushchev. Instead, I concentrated on outlining, summing up, and projecting into the future the broad social trends at work in contemporary Russia. This led me to the conclusion that the Soviet Union was approaching a critical turn of its history at which it would be compelled to begin to move in a new direction, and that Stalin's death, far from being the main cause of the change, would merely speed it up and underline its inevitability.

My analysis and conclusions have become the subjects of an animated controversy on both sides of the Atlantic.

It is hardly surprising that some of my fiercest critics are precisely those luckless soothsayers who either had already seen Beria in Stalin's place, or had been quite sure of the 'absolute ideological solidarity' of Stalin's heirs. I have also drawn the wrath of the professional propagandists of the cold war, and quite especially of the anti-communist crusaders fighting under the lofty banners of the 'Congress for Cultural Freedom'. On the other hand, many serious and able writers have defended my views with much conviction and effect. This controversy has already found its echoes, both friendly and hostile, in the French Press as well; and I propose to deal here especially with M. Raymond Aron's extensive critique of my views which appeared in the October issue of *Preuves*. . . .

Any realistic analysis of the Stalin era and of its conclusion must draw a balance of the Soviet industrial revolution of the last twenty-five years, the revolution by force of which Russia has from one of the industrially most backward nations become the world's second industrial power. This process was accompanied by vast educational progress, into which the bulk of Soviet society has been drawn. Stalinist despotism and terrorism drove the Soviet people to carry through this industrial revolution, in part despite themselves, at an unprecedented pace, and in the face of unprecedented difficulties. The 'primitive magic of Stalinism' reflected the cultural backwardness of Soviet society in the formative years and in the middle stretches of the Stalin era. From this argument I concluded that with the progress achieved in the 1950's, the Stalinist terrorism and primitive magic had outlived their day and were coming into conflict with the new needs of Soviet society. The higher level of industrial and general civilization favoured a gradual democratization of Soviet political life, although a military dictatorship, of the Bonapartist type, might also arise amid mounting international tensions. Both these prospects signify an end to Stalinism. An attempt to galvanize the Stalinist régime and orthodoxy was still possible and even probable; but it could hardly meet with more than episodic success.

The cold war propagandist bases all his arguments and slogans on the assumption of an unchangeable and irredeemable evil in Stalinism or communism at large. Remove that evil, and all his ideological thrusts strike into a vacuum. He therefore stubbornly refuses to see that the 'evil' has been historically determined and that the profound transformation of the structure and outlook of Soviet society cannot fail to have far-reaching political consequences.

At this point my critics, especially M. Raymond Aron, accuse me of all the mortal sins of Marxist determinism: I am said to deny the importance of human will in history; to eliminate the role of the individual, especially that of the *grand homme* and leader; and to ascribe one-sidedly to the economic structure of society that determining influence on human affairs which it does not and cannot possess.

I have, of course, never denied my Marxist convictions, but I try to stand on my own feet without leaning on Marx's much abused authority. As a matter of principle I have always endeavoured to develop my argument in such a way that its validity should not depend on any specifically Marxist assumptions. One need not be a Marxist at all to agree with me on the impact of the Soviet industrial revolution upon Soviet politics. It has not occurred to a single historian of the XIXth century, conservative or liberal, to ignore the impact of the English industrial revolution upon the politics of Victorian England. Not a single historian can ignore the connection between that revolution and the gradual broadening of the franchise, that is the gradual democratization of England. It is a truism that modern forms of democratic life have developed mainly in industrialized nations and have, as a rule, failed to develop in nations that have remained on the pre-industrial, semi-feudal level of civilization. But what is accepted as a truism in the modern and contemporary history of the non-communist world is, in the eyes of our critics, totally inapplicable to the Soviet Union: there it is simply preposterous to expect that massive industrialization, urbanization, and educational progress may foster any democratic trends and tendencies.

A few of the critics have put forward an argument which I am not inclined to dismiss out of hand. What about Germany? they ask. Has a high level of industrialization and mass education prevented Germany from producing the worst authoritarianism and totalitarianism? Did Nazism not have its 'primitive magic'? How can one speak about Russia 'outgrowing' Stalinism when Germany never really 'outgrew' Nazism, which was destroyed only from the outside, through war?

I ought, perhaps, to remark that I have nowhere said or suggested that industrialization and educational progress automatically guarantee a democratic development. All I have said is that industrialization *tends* to awaken democratic aspirations in the masses. These aspirations may, of course, be frustrated or defeated by other factors. But even in Germany industrialization did foster the democratic trend. The four decades between Bismarck's *Ausnahmegesetz* and Hitler's rise saw a very considerable expansion of the democratic forms of political life, at first under the Hohenzollern Empire and then under the Weimar Republic. The German working class was the chief factor of that democratization—it wrested one democratic concession after another from its ruling classes. That it was not persistent and that it abdicated at the decisive moment, in 1933, does not obliterate the historical connection, evident even in Germany, between industrialization and democratic politics.

What Germany's history proves is this: the democratic trend was strong while German society was growing and expanding on a capitalist basis. It withered and gave place to the totalitarian trend in a decaying society based on a shrinking capitalist economy, such as Germany's economy was on the eve of Hitler's rise. Unemployment of millions, an all-pervading sense of social instability, mass fear and mass hysteria, these were the basic elements that went into the making of Nazism. In addition there was the envy, the hatred, and the contempt of the *Kleinbürgertum* for the labour movement; the illusion of that *Kleinbürgertum* that it could assert itself against both the *Grossbürgertum* and the proletariat; the determination of the German industrial and financial barons to use the lower middle class run amok against the proletariat; the internal division and impotence of German labour; and—last but not least— Germany's national pride wounded since the 1918 defeat and her acute craving for revenge. This was the specific and very complex combination of factors which produced the particular German brand of a totalitarian régime on the basis of a capitalist economy.

While it is obviously true that a high industrial civilization does not preclude the growth of totalitarianism, it should be even more obvious that it is not that civilization *per se* which is responsible for that growth. In each case the specific causes of totalitarianism must be examined. I have tried to expose the specific sources of Stalinism in the state of Soviet society of the 1920's, and to show that these sources have been drying up in the 1950's. It is therefore no answer to say that from very different sources, namely from the ferments of the German society of the 1920's and 1930's, there came something that was outwardly, and only outwardly, very similar to Stalinism. I insist on the analysis of specific causes and consequences, while my critics reason very much like that old Polish peasant who argued with his children that it was useless to cure tuberculosis in the family, because, having cured tuberculosis, they would die from some epidemics sooner or later. I maintain that urbanization and modernization are 'curing' the Soviet Union from Stalinism. 'But think of the epidemic of Nazism,' some profound thinkers reply, 'to which Germany succumbed; and in view of it how can one speak about Russia curing herself of Stalinism?'

Certainly, if conditions like those that gave rise to Nazism—mass unemployment, a shrinking economy, a sense of social insecurity, national humiliation, fear, and mass hysteria—were to appear in the Soviet Union, the result would probably be very similar. However, even my critics do not expect such conditions to arise in the Soviet Union within the foreseeable future. (Such conditions might appear in consequence of Russia's defeat in a third world war, and the result would certainly be not democracy but some form of a fascist totalitarianism, if these political terms were still to retain any meaning after an atomic war.)

It can never be sufficiently strongly emphasized that Soviet society, no matter whether one views it with hostile or friendly eyes, or only openmindedly, cannot be understood at all if one of its basic characteristics is ignored, namely the fact that it is an expanding society and that it expands on the basis of a planned economy making it immune from that extreme economic and moral instability which in bourgeois society tends to produce fascist mass neuroses. The Soviet Union is emerging from Stalinism with all the conditions necessary for continued expansion, expansion not merely during certain phases of the industrial cycle or during armament booms. Continuous expansion is in fact inherent in planned economy of the socialist, or even of the present Soviet type, as the basic form of its movement, just as the ups and downs of the trade cycle represent the forms of movement peculiar to 'normal' capitalism. (This is the hard core of truth in all communist propaganda; and it is all too easy to overlook or rashly to reject it because it is usually wrapped up in thick layers of crude fiction.) Stalinist totalitarianism and primitive magic, belonging essentially to an earlier transitional period, become irrelevant, anachronistic, and untenable in this expanding society at its present level of productive forces. How much more irrelevant to the problems of that society are the phenomena of Nazism or fascism born from social decay and disintegration.

One of my French critics claims that in expounding this determinist view I am reducing '*le rôle de la volonté humaine*' and the role '*des grands hommes*' in history. I may perhaps be allowed to ask: reducing in relation to —what? To their actual role in the historical process? or to the critic's grossly exaggerated idea of that role? I certainly take the view that the human will is 'free' only to the extent to which it acts as the promoter of 'necessity', that is within limits circumscribed by conditions external to it. The will of the *grands hommes* represents only one particular case of the general problem of the human will: *le grand homme* 'makes' history within the limits which his environment and the existing balance of social forces, national or international, allow him to do so. My French critic seems flabbergasted at my suggestion that the Bolshevik revolution of 1917 could perhaps have taken place even without Lenin. He, on the contrary, sees Lenin as the sovereign maker of that revolution, and Lenin's personal role as more important than all 'objective trends', than the 'Spirit of the time', and the 'laws of history, and similar abstractions' (the use of some of which he ascribes to me altogether fortuitously). My French critic—M. Raymond Aron—is therefore quite consistent with himself when he writes: '*Peut-être aurait-il suffi que le train plombé qui transportait Lénine à travers l'Allemagne* [in 1917] *sautât ou que Trotsky fût retenu aux Etats-Unis ou en Angleterre, pour que l'Esprit du temps s'exprimât autrement.*' ['Perhaps it would have been enough had the sealed train which carried Lenin across Germany smashed up, or that Trotsky had been detained in the United States or England for the Spirit of the times to have expressed itself differently.'] Thus my critic takes us back to the

crude belief in the decisive role of the accident in history
—to the old quip that the history of the Roman Empire
would have been quite different if the shape of Cleo-
patra's nose had not been what it was—and also back to
Carlyle's idea of the 'hero in history', an idea perhaps
indispensable to fascism, Stalinism, and . . . Gaullism.
At this point I plead guilty: in relation to this view of
history I *do* reduce the role of the *volonté humaine*
and of *le grand homme*: I do not worship at their
temples.[1]

The extremely subjectivist and voluntarist approach
of most of my critics allows them, of course, to 'reduce
the role' of all objective circumstances, and more specifically to ignore the impact of economic processes, unprecedented in scope and momentum, upon the political, cultural, and moral future of the Soviet Union.
They see the whole of the Russian revolution in terms
of the bad faith or evil ambition, or 'Manichean-like'
moods of a few Bolshevik leaders. These evil intentions
or ambitions existed, of course, prior to the five Five
Year Plans; and they continue to operate into an indefinite future. They enable one to 'explain' the whole
development of the Soviet Union and of world communism as a single sequence of plots and conspiracies.
How was it that Stalin first imposed upon his party, by
fire and sword, the doctrine of 'socialism in one country',
that he compelled the whole of international communism to accept this doctrine, and that then he did more
than anyone else to contribute to the spread of communism to a dozen countries? Was this perhaps a deep,
and in a sense tragic contradiction of Stalinism, as I have
tried to prove?

Nothing of the sort, say my critics. Stalin's fanatical
preaching of 'socialism in one country' was either an
irrelevancy or a fraud meant to mislead the world, more

[1] Curiously enough, a critic in *The Times Literary Supplement*
(28 August 1953) thinks that I have 'tended to exaggerate the personal
elements inherent in Stalinism',

probably a fraud and a conspiracy. Like a certain type of anti-Semite who draws his inspiration from the 'Protocols of the Elders of Zion', so the cold war propagandist at heart believes in the existence of some 'Protocols of the Elders of Communism' which one day will no doubt be unearthed and revealed to the world. And then it will be proven that all doctrines of Stalinism and the bloody struggles over them were only so much make-believe designed to cover up the communist conspiracy against the world.

Some of the critics, especially Russian veteran Mensheviks and their American pupils, dismiss the idea of a democratic evolution in the Soviet Union or in the Communist Party, because any such idea fails to take into account how inseparable the totalitarian outlook has been from the Bolshevik Party: Bolshevik totalitarianism goes back allegedly to Lenin's fight over the party statutes in 1903, the year when the Russian socialists split into Bolsheviks and Mensheviks. Lenin then demanded that only active participants in the party's underground work should be recognized as party members, whereas the Mensheviks wished to grant membership to 'sympathizers' as well. It was then, we are told, that the issue was decided in advance, the issue which looms behind the great upheavals of this century, behind the sequence of revolution and counter-revolution, behind the massive reality of Stalinist totalitarianism, behind the cold war, and behind the dangers now threatening the world. All these have their origin in that idea about party organization which Lenin embodied in his first paragraph of the party statutes over fifty years ago. Thus half a century of Russian and even world history is seen as springing from Lenin's head, from a single idea in his brain. Should one really carry one's contempt for 'materialist determinism' as far as that?

The cold war propagandist conceals, cleverly and not so cleverly, his intellectual embarrassment or helplessness with the terms 'totalitarianism' and 'totalitarian'.

Whenever he is unable or mentally too lazy to explain a phenomenon, he resorts to that label. . . .

> *Denn eben wo Begriffe fehlen*
> *Da stellt zur rechten Zeit ein Wort sich ein.*
> *Mit Worten lässt sich trefflich streiten,*
> *Mit Worten ein System bereiten.*

I should perhaps explain that I myself have occasionally applied this term to describe certain aspects of Stalinism—I have been doing this at least since 1932. But the term should be used carefully and sparingly. Nothing is more confusing and harmful than the habit of lumping together diverse régimes and social phenomena under one label. Stalinists have often lumped together all their opponents as fascists. The anti-Stalinist lumps together Nazis, fascists, Stalinists, Leninists, and just Marxists, as totalitarians, and then assures us that totalitarianism, being a completely new phenomenon, rules out even the possibility of any change and evolution, let alone quasi-liberal reform. A totalitarian régime, he claims, can never be reformed or overthrown from inside; it can be destroyed from the outside only, by force of arms, as Hitler's régime was.

The fact is that nearly all modern revolutions (the Paris Commune, the Russian revolutions of 1905 and 1917, the Central European revolutions of 1918, the Chinese revolution of 1948-9) and even most democratic reforms, have come in the wake of war and military defeat, not as a result of purely internal developments; and this has been so even in non-totalitarian régimes. Yet it would be a striking mistake to treat totalitarianism metaphysically as a state of society's utter immobility, or of history's absolute freezing, which excludes any political movement in the form of action from below or reform from above. It is true, of course, that the chances of such action or reform were negligible under Stalin. But they have grown enormously since the critical moment, at the end of the Stalin era, when the crisis in leadership coincided with the accumulation of changes in the depth of society. In denying this, my critics imperceptibly abandon their extreme opposition to determinism and themselves adopt an utterly unrealistic brand of determinism. They, too, argue now that Russia's political future is predetermined, only that it is not the economic and cultural data—the fact that the Russian steppes and the wastes of Siberia are covered by thousands of new factories, that Russia's urban population has grown by over 40 million souls within a little more than twenty years, or that proportionately more young people attend schools in Russia than anywhere else in the world—it is not these facts that can determine Russia's political future, in the critics' view. It is the politics of the Stalin era and they alone—the single party system, the absence of free discussion, the leader cult, the terror of the political police, and so on—that are going to decide the shape of things to come. Their 'determinism' amounts to this: politics is determined by politics alone, it is self-sufficient and independent of other fields of social life. To be sure, in my view the economic processes are of primary importance, but they are closely connected with cultural developments and the moral climate; they are dependent on the political circumstances and themselves have a powerful impact on those circumstances. The critics' pseudo-determinism is one-dimensional, whereas the much abused and 'old-fashioned' Marxist determinism has at least the advantage that it tries to grasp reality as it is: multi-dimensional in all its aspects and dynamic.

A certain type of 'left-wing' cold war propagandist, who has not yet had the time to shed the *infantile diseases of ex-communism*, approaches the issue from a 'Marxist' angle, and turns against my analysis the 'weapon' of economic determinism. A break with the Stalin era and a democratic evolution, he argues, are excluded because they would go against the class or group interest of the privileged and ruling minority of Soviet society. The argument, be it noted, was first advanced partially by Trotsky, although Trotsky cannot be held responsible for the oversimplifications of the Trotskyites.

The managerial and bureaucratic class, it is said, has a vested interest in maintaining the economic and social inequality of the Stalin era. It must therefore preserve the whole apparatus of coercion and terror which enforces that inequality.

This argument assumes:

(*a*) that there exists a high degree of something like class solidarity in the Soviet bureaucratic and managerial groups; and

(*b*) that the ruling group is guided in its policies by a strong awareness of, and concern for, the distinct class interest of the privileged.

These assumptions may or may not be correct—in my view the evidence is still inconclusive. A weighty argument against them is that we have repeatedly seen the privileged and ruling minority of Soviet society deeply divided against itself and engaged in a ferocious struggle ending with the extermination of large sections of the bureaucracy. The victims of the mass purges of 1936–8 came mainly from the party cadres, the managerial groups, and the military officers' corps, and only in the last instance from the non-privileged masses. Whether these purges accelerated the social integration of the new privileged minority, or whether, on the contrary, they prevented that minority from forming itself into a solid social stratum is, I admit, still an open question to me.

In any case, we cannot say beforehand to what degree the privileged groups may resist any democratic-socialist and egalitarian trend emerging in Soviet society. It may be that they will defend their privileges tooth and nail and fight any such trend with stubborn cruelty. But it is at least quite as possible that the 'class solidarity' of the privileged minority should prove weak, that its resistance to the democratic-socialist trend should prove half-hearted and ineffective, and that the first impulse for quasi-liberal reforms should come, as it has already come, from the ranks of the bureaucracy itself. This is not to say that one ought to expect democratization to be brought about exclusively by reform from above: a combination of pressure from below and reform from above may be necessary. Yet at a certain stage of development it is the quasi-liberal reform from above that may most effectively spur on a revival of spontaneous political action below or create the conditions under which such action may become possible after a whole epoch of totalitarian torpor.

But even if we assume, for the sake of the argument, that Soviet bureaucracy does represent a single social and political interest, it would still not follow that that interest must lie in the perpetuation of the extreme inequality and oppression of the Stalin era. That inequality was the direct outcome of a poverty of available resources which did not permit not merely an egalitarian distribution but even a distant approach to egalitarianism. As I have pointed out at greater length in *Russia After Stalin*, a strong differentiation of incomes was the only way in which Russia could develop her resources sufficiently to overcome that initial poverty. In other words, the privileges of the managerial and bureaucratic groups coincided with a broader national interest. Yet, with the growth of productive forces, which makes possible an alleviation of the still existing poverty in consumer goods, a reduction of inequality becomes possible, desirable, and even necessary for the further development of the nation's wealth and civilization. Such a reduction need not take place primarily or mainly through the lowering of the standards of living of the privileged minority, but through the raising of the standards of the majority. In a stagnant society, living on a national income the size of which remains stationary over the years, the standard of living of the broad masses cannot be improved otherwise than at the expense of the privileged groups, who therefore resist any attempt at such improvement. But in a society living on a rapidly growing national income, the privileged groups need not pay, or need not pay heavily, for the rise in the well-being of the working masses; and so they need not necessarily oppose the rise.

The privileged minority in the U.S.S.R. has no *absolute* interest—it may still have a relative and a temporary one—in perpetuating the economic discrepancies and social antagonisms that were inevitable at a lower level of economic development. Nor need they cling to a political régime designed to suppress and conceal those antagonisms behind a 'monolithic' façade. Stalinism, with its orthodoxy, its iron curtain, and its elaborate political mythology, kept the Soviet people more or less in the dark about the scope and depth of its own social divisions and cleavages. But with the phenomenal growth of Soviet wealth these divisions tend to become softened; and the orthodoxy, the iron curtain, and the elaborate mythology of Stalinism *tend* to become socially useless. Only inertia may still keep them in being for a time, but the inertia is bound to spend itself; and the open-eyed observer of the Soviet scene can hardly fail to see that it is already beginning to spend itself.

More than at any previous time in history the political evolution of nations depends now on international as much as on internal factors. Nowhere in the world does the danger and fear of war strengthen democratic institutions. It would be idle to expect that any democratic trend in the U.S.S.R., which would, in any case, have to contend against so much resistance, could be strengthened while a war-like mood prevailed in and outside the Soviet Union. Any further growth of international tension would most probably arrest the democratic trend and stimulate a new form of authoritarianism or totalitarianism. Since the Stalinist form has outlived its relative historic justification and since danger of war enhances the already strong position of the armed forces, that new authoritarianism or totalitarianism is likely to assume a Bonapartist form. A Soviet version of Bonapartism would in its turn increase the danger of war or perhaps make war unavoidable.

This trend of thought seems to have come as a shock to my critic. M. Aron whom I have already quoted poses a question: '*Pourquoi un régime Bonapartiste signifierait-il la guerre? Un général, qui s'efforcerait de liquider le terrorisme du parti, serait normalement enclin à un accord avec l'Occident.*' ['Why should a Bonapartist régime mean war? A general who tried to end the terrorism of the party would normally incline towards the West.'] I re-read these sentences and rub my eyes: is it possible that they should have been written by a Frenchman, and a French 'political philosopher'? '*Pourquoi un régime Bonapartiste signifierait-il la guerre?*' Why indeed *did* it signify that? And why does the assumption that a similar régime in Russia would also signify war seem so far-fetched? Because a general 'liquidating the terrorism of the party' should in fact be peacefully minded. But—the question must be asked—was not the domestic terrorism of the Jacobin party finally liquidated under Napoleon? And did not Napoleon project in a sense that terrorism on to the international arena?

No matter to what historical school we belong, Bonapartist or anti-Bonapartist, pro- or anti-Jacobin, we cannot deny the seeming paradox that, for all their domestic terrorism, the Jacobins conducted their foreign policy much more pacifically than Napoleon did, who in domestic affairs stood for law and order. Did not the warning against carrying revolution abroad on the point of bayonets come from Danton and Robespierre, the revolutionary terrorists? The Jacobins suppressed by means of the guillotine the domestic tensions which the revolution had brought into the open or had created, while Napoleon could deal with those tensions only by finding foreign outlets for them. To be sure, this was only one aspect of the problem—the other was the attitude of counter-revolutionary Europe and England—but it was a most essential aspect.

It will now perhaps be seen why a Russian analogy to this is not altogether unreal: A Russian general or marshal may install himself in the Kremlin, 'liquidate the terrorism of the party', and have the most peaceful intentions towards the outside world. But his intentions may carry little weight compared with the circumstances in which he has assumed power. He will have inherited the most severe strains and stresses from the Stalinist or post-Stalinist régime. There will be tensions between town and country, between collectivism and individualism in the countryside, and between Russia proper, the Ukraine, Georgia, and the other outlying Republics. Stalinism had almost continually suppressed these tensions by terroristic methods. This was precisely why it was on the whole pacific in its foreign policy. Stalin was preoccupied with his domestic problems; and his manner of dealing with them was such that, never being quite free from those preoccupations, he had to maintain an essentially defensive attitude towards the outside world. In 1948–52, when Russia's immediate military pre-eminence in Europe was undeniable, a Russian Bonaparte might have issued marching orders to the Soviet army—Stalin, despite his 'Manichean-like attitude' and 'messianic fervour', did not. Whatever the clichés of vulgar history writing and propaganda may say about this, Stalin's domestic terrorism and cautious, 'peace-loving' foreign policy were only two sides of the same medal.

If a Soviet marshal were to take power, he would do so under conditions of domestic disorder and acute international tension—in a more normal situation he would hardly have a chance. He would either find the apparatus of Stalinist terrorism smashed or he himself would have to smash it in order to justify himself. He would thus be deprived of the old means for controlling and suppressing domestic tensions. The dangerous international situation would hardly allow him to deal with those tensions in a patient, slow, reformist manner.

Instability and insecurity at home would impart an explosive character to his foreign policy—he would be impelled to find foreign outlets for domestic tensions. Having started out with the establishment of law and order at home and with the most peaceful intentions towards the outside world, the Russian Bonaparte, like his French prototype, would be driven into unpredictable military adventure, in part because he would not be able to exercise domestic control through intense terrorism. He would probably prove to be just as much more bellicose than Stalin and Molotov and Malenkov as Napoleon proved to be more bellicose than Robespierre and Danton.

I admit that I remain a determinist on this point: the ultimate course upon which a Soviet Bonaparte would embark would not greatly depend on his assumed personal inclination to come to terms with the West. He might be inspired by the most pacific intentions; he might even have his Peace of Amiens (over the meaning of which generations of historians would later argue); and yet he would in all probability be driven to war, even 'aggressive' war, by a combination of international and domestic factors.

My critics' approach is more often than not dictated by their prejudice against Bolshevism in all its phases, pre-Stalinist, Stalinist, and post-Stalinist. From this prejudice they engage in ludicrously belated apologetics for Tsardom and argue at length about the progressive features of the Tsarist régime, which, if only it had existed till now, would have taken Russia much further ahead on the road of industrial and cultural progress than the Bolshevik revolution has done. From the same prejudice they are prepared to hail the advent of a Soviet Bonaparte. 'Anybody, anybody is preferable to the Bolsheviks!' seems to be the maxim. Any talk about the proletarian democratic element in Bolshevism—an element strongly submerged yet genuine—seems to the critics to defy reality. Yet the vision of the angel of peace dressed up in the uniform of the Russian Bonaparte does not at all seem odd to them.

The alternative is still between a democratic evolution of communism and some sort of a military dictatorship. This, it seems to me, is the basic, the *long-term* alternative. It has never occurred to me that the historic choice will be made very soon after Stalin's death. At any rate, the full 'liberalization' of the régime or the full resurgence of the proletarian democratic tradition of communism could not be a matter of a few months or even years. What the events that followed immediately after Stalin's death could show and have shown is that the alternative outlined above is real, and that the impulses that may push the Soviet Union in one direction or the other are already at work and are already in conflict with one another. The long-term character of the prognostication frees me from the need to reply any further to those critics who point to the events of a few months to conclude that my forecast has been refuted. I can only express mild surprise at this naïve disregard of the time factor.

This is not to say that we can ignore the connection between the short-term and the long-term developments, or that we have fixed our eyes so exclusively on the latter that the former have caught us unawares. My prognostication made allowance for the short-term prospects as well. In *Russia After Stalin* I wrote that besides the basic alternative—military dictatorship versus socialist democracy—there was still the possibility of 'a relapse into the Stalinist form of dictatorship'. I added: 'A *prolonged* relapse into Stalinism is highly improbable' (p. 159 of the English edition). The adjective 'prolonged', italicized in the original, pointed directly, though perhaps too laconically, to the probability of a *short* relapse. Something like it has in the meantime occurred and is still in progress—but even this relapse has been only partial and vague and feeble, and it is being carefully concealed.

History has only opened a new chapter on Russia—let us patiently watch her as she fills the pages.

POST-STALINIST FERMENT
OF IDEAS[1]

THE ferment of ideas in Russia which has come to
the surface since Stalin's death continues to develop.
For more than a year the Russian intelligentsia have been
plunged in a controversy, the like of which they had not
known for nearly a quarter of a century. Scientists, men
of letters, artists, educationists, all have argued the issues
which preoccupy them; and they have sometimes done
this with a zest which shows them to be, after all, the
descendants of the old Russian revolutionary intelligentsia. Behind the controversy there have been
attempts, some audacious and others timid, at a 'transvaluation of the values' inherited from the Stalin era.

It is in this triumph, be it even temporary, of controversy over conformity that Russia's break with the
Stalin era may be seen most clearly at present. This is no
more a matter of calculated, mechanical moves made by
party bosses, politicians, and diplomats, moves of which
it may still be said that they point to no significant change
in the political framework or the social background of
the Soviet Union. When some of the accepted standards
of thought and behaviour and some of the sacrosanct
axioms of Stalinism are emphatically and even vehemently questioned by scientists, authors, artists, and
even party spokesmen, when the whole of the Russian
intelligentsia are engaged in restless and dangerous
heart-searching, it is no longer possible to doubt that
the urge for change and reform is strongly at work

[1] A shortened version of this essay appeared in *The Times* in November 1954 and gave rise to a considerable controversy in its correspondence columns.

and only those who know little about Russia's history can still argue that the intellectual ferment has little or no bearing on Russia's practical politics.

What could be heard in all the recent debates has been a protest of the Soviet intelligentsia against the mental sterility and mediocrity to which Stalinism had condemned them. Economists have vented their resentment at an orthodoxy under which they were reduced to the role of Stalin's gramophone records. Biologists have reacted against the humiliation they had suffered at Lysenko's hands. Physicists have declared that they have had enough of the chauvinistic Great Russian swank, which was *en vogue* until recently, and of isolation from Western science. Painters and sculptors have revolted against that 'socialist realism' which has compelled them to dress, in shoddy style, Stalin and his entourage as demi-gods. Novelists and poets have expressed disgust at the patterns into which thought control had sought to constrict their creative imagination, at the compulsion to produce dramas without real conflict, novels without living people, and lyrical poetry without genuine feeling. 'We have had enough of your Stalin Prizes and of the fantastic fees and of privileges corrupting us and our minds', some of them have cried out publicly. The youth of Russia, the students of the Universities of Moscow, Leningrad, and Kiev, have rebelled against the hypocrisy and rigid formalism of the Stalin cult. Two generations have joined hands in this movement: old people who have borne the burden of Stalinist orthodoxy in fear and meekness during the greater part of their lives; and the young ones who are straining to throw off that burden at the threshold of adult life. Even in the concentration camps in the Polar regions, if recent ex-inmates are to be believed, the deportees have formed themselves into distinct groups, produced their political programmes and blueprints for the future, and argued among themselves, something they had not done in the course of about twenty years.

The attitude of Stalin's successors towards these developments is equivocal. Two souls seem to dwell in the breast of the Malenkov government. It was that government itself which initiated the present heart-searching when it buried the Stalin cult together with Stalin, when it ordered party propagandists to launch the attack against the 'un-Marxist cult of the single leader', when it intimated to the people that the time had come to do away with the totems and taboos of the Stalin era, when it threw into dramatic relief Stalin's failures in various fields of policy, and when it thrust open the heavy gates of the Kremlin to the man in the street and to the youth of Russia. The intelligentsia have taken all these gestures and hints as a promise of a new era, an encouragement and a challenge to their thought, courage, and dignity. Not for nothing did Ilya Ehrenburg call his new and controversial novel *The Thaw*.

Stalin's closest associates and successors were indeed the first to break the ice. But soon they began to wonder in perplexity whither the drifting floes might not carry them. They had done away with the Stalin cult, by which they themselves had been oppressed, with a sigh of relief but also with mental reservations. Malenkov, Khrushchev, and Molotov, not to speak of Beria, had owed their positions of power to Stalin. In varying degrees they had all been his accomplices. A frank and a radical disavowal of Stalinism would threaten to bring discredit upon their own heads. They cannot allow the Soviet people to know the full truth about the Stalin era. They cannot drag the corpse of their Master through the mud and at the same time save their own faces. Having at first quietly abandoned the cult, they could not then but seek to salve its wreckage. Having sneaked away from Stalinist orthodoxy, they cannot but try to sneak back to it.

Their dilemma is not, however, determined by these considerations alone. There are in the Stalinist heritage important elements which no communist government could renounce, not even one consisting of men altogether untainted by Stalinism, if such a government were possible. Moreover, no anti-communist government could renounce them either. None could dismantle the planned economy set up under Stalin, or allow the peasants to leave *en masse* the collective farms and restore smallholdings, without condemning Russia to chaos, misery, and famine (as this writer has argued in greater detail in one of his recent books). Stalin's successors are, of course, explicitly committed to preserve and develop these elements of the Stalinist heritage.

Here is the deeper source of most of their dilemmas. The present social structure of the Soviet Union is already established too firmly to be undone, but not yet firmly enough to function altogether of its own accord, without coercion from above. It no longer needs for its survival all the totalitarian discipline by which it was set up, but it cannot altogether dispense with that discipline. Malenkov's government has tried to find, by trial and error, a new balance between coercion and persuasion. It has relaxed the Stalinist discipline, but it watches anxiously to see whether the discontents and ferments released thereby are not growing into a menace to both the structure of society and the position of the ruling group. The controversy in the ranks of the intelligentsia and the official reactions to it are symptomatic of this complex situation.

The road back to Stalinist orthodoxy and discipline is barred, because that orthodoxy and discipline belong to an epoch which has come to a close. They fitted an essentially primitive, pre-industrial society engaged in feverish industrialization and collectivization. They resulted from the attempt to impose on the Russia of *muzhiks* an ideal and a way of life for which that Russia was not prepared, either materially or mentally. The primitive magic of Stalinism, the deification of the Leader, and the bizarre and elaborate rituals of Stalinism had all sprung from Russian backwardness and all served to tame that backwardness. Since the vast and swift transformation of the whole social outlook of Russia, undertaken by Stalin, was not based on the will and understanding of the people, its origin had to be traced to the superhuman wisdom and will of the Leader. Opposition was branded as the Devil's work, especially when it was inspired by the Marxist tradition which was irreconcilable with the cult of the Leader and the primitive magic. Throughout the Stalin era the rulers, the ideologists, and the policemen, too, were constantly engaged in turning the modern conceptions of Marxism into the idiom of primitive magic and in translating the do's and don't's of that magic into the vocabulary of Marxism.

After decades of this ideological diet, the Soviet intelligentsia are visibly suffering from moral nausea. This is a very different intelligentsia from that which witnessed Stalin's ascendancy. Their background is not the inert and helpless Russia of the *muzhik* 'but the second industrial power of the world which has reached the threshold of the atomic age almost simultaneously with the United States. To be sure, much of the old primitivism and barbarism remains embedded in Russian life. But while the old intelligentsia suffered acutely from the discrepancy between their own intellectual progress and the nation's poverty and backwardness, the present generation of the intelligentsia suffers even more acutely from the contrast between the nation's material progress and the backwardness of its spiritual climate.

This state of affairs concerns Soviet society as a whole, not merely the intelligentsia. The working of the national economy, the functioning of social institutions, and the efficiency of administration are affected by it no less than academic life, literature, and the arts. The monolithic thought-control, which Stalinism had used to force through industrialization and collectivization and to make Soviet society accept all the attendant miseries, has now become a formidable obstacle to further progress in technology, government, and social organization. Having for decades lived under its own (triumphant!) brand of McCarthyism with its loyalty tests, charges of un-Bolshevik activities, witch-hunts and purges, terroristic suspicion and suspicious terrorism, Soviet society is now driven by self-preservation to try and regain initiative and freedom of decision and action. Too many of its public men, civil servants, scientists, intellectuals, and workers have become cowed and intimidated creatures devoid of creative aspiration and ambition. What is surprising under the circumstances is not Russia's failures but Russia's achievements in so many fields. It is a fact that not long ago some of Russia's best aircraft constructors, for instance, designed their best engines in prison cells and places of exile; and their lot was almost symbolical for the condition under which Russia's creative energies sought to assert themselves under Stalinism.

But a modern industrial nation cannot allow its creative energies to be so constricted, unless it is prepared to pay the penalty of ultimate stagnation. The more a nation is technologically advanced the greater is the danger, because its very existence depends on the freedom of its technologists and administrators to exercise their abilities and judgment. The needs of Russia's development are now in a much more direct and dramatic conflict with the Stalinist magic than ever before. The aircraft designers must be let out of the prisons, literally and metaphorically, if Russian aircraft design is to meet the demands which the international armament race, to mention only this, makes on it. The biologists have to be allowed freedom of research if farming is to make good its long lag behind the rest of the economy. Industrial managers must be released from the fetters of that Stalinist super-centralism which was still tolerable on a lower and less complex level of industrialization, when the Politbureau could still have some insight into the affairs of every major industrial concern and settle them by its fiat. Nor can the mass of skilled industrial workers be kept in a condition of semi-serfdom if the efficiency of their labour is to rise. And, last but not least, authors, artists, and journalists must be unmuzzled if the moral gulf between the rulers and the ruled is to be bridged or narrowed. This is why Stalin's successors cannot easily go on enforcing the old discipline, no matter how much they may be afraid of the consequences of relaxation.

The twists and turns of their policy are reflected in the recent fortunes of the Stalin cult. For months after Stalin had died his name was not mentioned publicly. The silence about him could not have been deeper if he had died a hundred years earlier; and its meaning was underlined by the emphatic denunciations of the 'un-Marxist cult of the single leader'.

But there was something unreal and awkward in that silence. There was in it a sense of tension and embarrassment which came from the fact that the new skeleton in the Soviet cupboard was the omnipresent deity of yesterday. After a lapse of time Stalin began to be mentioned once again, as if casually, by the propagandists. Discreet reminders followed of his merits so quickly forgotten. Then he was stealthily half-restored to the apostolic succession of Marx-Engels-Lenin. Even now, however, the place accorded to him in the historical retrospects, which are constantly drawn and redrawn and retouched, is not more than a modest footnote to the epic story of Lenin, the revolution, and the Soviet State. Salvaged from the refuse heap, soiled and defaced, Stalin's figure has been granted a new but rather meagre allowance of ideological respectability. These posthumous vicissitudes of the Stalin cult, so comic to the outsider, are gravely portentous to the Soviet citizen to whom they indicate how far he is, or is not, allowed to drift away from the old orthodoxy and discipline.

The debunking of Stalinism is now evidently under a ban. But quietly the departure from Stalinism continues in many fields. Where orthodoxy hampers technological progress and economic efficiency, the canons of Stalinism are being jettisoned without much ado. At the same time the reaction against Stalinism is being curbed and discouraged in those fields where it may directly impinge upon the political stability of the régime. But it is not easy to draw a line between social efficiency and political expediency, because often their requirements conflict with one another.

Perhaps the most important reform has just been decreed in education. Not only has the Stalin cult, which has clogged all processes of education, been played down. The educational system is in addition being freed from the grip of authoritarianism, and pedagogy is encouraged to take up again those experimental and more libertarian conceptions which animated the Soviet school in the early years of the Soviet régime. Under Stalin the educational system gave the pupil, apart from technical training and *Politgramota* ('political literacy'), the habits of unquestioning obedience. The relation of teacher to pupil was one of old-fashioned paternalism, a reflection of Stalin's own paternalistic attitude towards 'his' people. Austere classroom discipline, obligatory uniforms, a multiplicity of severe and highly formal examinations had made the Stalinist school almost undistinguishable, in the manner and style of the teaching, from the school and seminary of the Tsarist era. Coeducation was, of course, frowned upon and eventually forbidden. The ghost of Pobedonostsev, the famous reactionary ideologue, seemed to stalk the schoolrooms and smile with malignant contentment.

Under the new reform coeducation has been rehabilitated and reintroduced. The curriculum has been broadened and made less rigid. The number of examinations is substantially reduced, and school discipline is to be less formal. The paternalistic system is giving place to one in which more emphasis is placed on the formation in the pupil of an independent mind and character.

And, after an interval of nearly a quarter of a century, the Soviet school is now resuming the experiment in 'polytechnical education', which aims at bringing the classroom close to the industrial workshop and the farm, and at combining brain work with manual labour. When the experiment was tried out in the early years of the Soviet régime it failed in part because 'polytechnical' education requires for its success a highly modern industrial background and environment which was still lacking. In addition Stalin viewed the polytechnical school with suspicion and hostility because of its modernistic and anti-authoritarian outlook. Post-Stalin Russia needs an educational system more modern and free than that bequeathed by Stalinism; and even though such a system may become the breeding ground of political ferment, the dictates of efficiency seem to have prevailed in this case over those of political expediency.

Changes are also introduced in 'inner party education', that is in the methods by which the collective mind of the party is shaped. Stalinist techniques of indoctrination are being partly abandoned in favour of a more sober and open-minded propagation of pristine Marxism-Leninism, as Stalin's successors understand it. To people in the West, inclined to lump together all these *isms*, the difference may seem too subtle to be of practical political significance. To Soviet citizens, however, the idea of a restoration of original Marxism-Leninism has a peculiar appeal, comparable perhaps to that which the Protestant rediscovery of the Bible once had to Western Europeans surfeited with the scholasticism of medieval theology. During the Stalin era an 'exaggerated' devotion to Marx and Lenin tended to mark a party member as a heretic. The Marxist classics were read, as a rule, in pre-digested excerpts and under the guidance of official commentators. During the great purges of the 1930's Stalin even issued a formal ban on the 'individual' study of Marx by party members. The reading of Marx's works was allowed only within the party's study circles; and attendance at those circles was compulsory for party members. Stalin felt that the individual study of Marxist classics induced in the student an attitude of independent inquiry critical of accepted truths; and he devised rules of party indoctrination which left the member with no time and opportunity for brooding over the texts and drawing his own conclusions. Marx had 'sown dragons'; and Stalin needed sheep.

Stalin's successors can hardly wish to raise a new breed of dragons; but they have not much use for the Stalinist sheep either. Compulsory indoctrination through party cells and study circles is abolished—attendance at those circles is henceforth optional. Party members are allowed and encouraged to study Marxist literature and party history in private. An all-round attempt is made to free 'ideological training' from canonical rigidity and to impart to it a somewhat more modern and businesslike style, although it is extremely difficult to eradicate from the party's mind (including the mind of its instructors) the ecclesiastical stamp which Stalinism had left on it.

The new outlook has been most remarkable in academic life, especially in those branches of science the teaching of which has the most direct bearing on economic efficiency. Already the appointment last year of G. Alexandrov to the post of Minister of Culture augured a new departure. At the height of the Zhdanov period Alexandrov had been dismissed from his post as the chief officer for ideological instruction and he remained eclipsed till the end of the Stalin era. In his *History of Philosophy* he had allegedly sinned with 'objectivism' and 'kowtowing' before Western philosophy. In truth, his *History* was written well within the party tradition, but as an academic textbook it baldly but objectively, without the admixture of much polemical invective, outlined the main trends of classical and modern philosophy. This was an unpardonable offence only a short time ago. Alexandrov's appointment to the Ministry of Culture foreshadowed therefore encouragement for conscientious academic inquiry, a break with the glorification of all things Russian, and also a sound reappraisal of the achievements of Western science.

The reappraisal has since found its expression in a series of debates on the fundamentals of philosophy and science which are still in progress in all Soviet seats of learning, and in the scholarly periodicals, from where the controversy has overspilled into the national Press. Recently, for instance, an eminent Academician, Professor S. L. Sobolev, surveyed in *Pravda* the problems of Russian academic life in terms which amounted to a severe indictment of the Stalin era and to a fervent plea for the restoration of intellectual integrity. The glorification of all things Russian and the drive against 'kowtowing before the West' had, according to Sobolev, led Soviet academic bodies to 'ignore the new physics' developed in the West. Sobolev castigated the obscurantist attitude prevalent until recently towards the work of Einstein, for which Lenin had shown high respect and intense interest, regardless of Einstein's 'naïvety in matters of pure philosophy'. Ridiculing the attempts to 'annihilate the theory of relativity', Sobolev writes: 'To us are dear also the names of the scientists of all countries. . . .' 'The most interesting discoveries . . . are always connected with the renunciation of pre-conceived ideas and with the audacious breaking of old norms and notions.' 'The clash of opinions and freedom of criticism are the most important pre-requisites of scientific progress.' 'The dogmatic attitude which substitutes fixed propositions for genuine research is the mortal enemy. . . . Our academic circles are still far from having lived down that attitude. . . . Some trends and works are given testimonials of political loyalty. Others . . . get the standard labels "reactionary" or 'idealistic".' This is only one of the very many voices which could be heard recently pleading for the abandonment of the black-and-white approach and for the revival of the art of fair and dispassionate debate.

In the course of this controversy more problems may well arise than its initiators had intended to pose. When *Pravda* readers are told that the 'clash of opinions and freedom of criticism are the most important pre-requisites of the development of science' they may well reflect whether this applies to social and political sciences as well, and to politics itself. In those fields there has been almost no sign of any 'clash of opinions' or freedom of criticism. True, the political outlook, too, is more sober and rational than it was in Stalin's days, but it continues to be 'monolithic'. Stalin's successors are evidently determined to keep politics insulated from the ferment of ideas. They appeal to the party to exercise its 'collective judgment', to rely on no single leader, and to revive 'inner party democracy'. But, like some of the characters in Tolstoy's *War and Peace*, who criticizing the Tsar's policy always instinctively stopped just at the point where they might seem to reflect on the Tsar himself and on autocracy, so the party spokesmen always stop at the point where the logic of their own arguments might lead them to plead for the right of the rank and file to dissent from the policies of the leaders and to seek a change in the party leadership.

The politically minded citizen finds, however, a sort of a substitute for political controversy in recent literary debates. Something like an explosion of discontent occurred in literary circles soon after Stalin's death. The distance between literature and politics is, and has always been, extremely short in Russia, where art for art's sake has never found much response. Russians have always expected their novelists, and poets, and literary critics to act as their social conscience and to produce the political message of their time. Only very few of the great writers have failed to meet that expectation. Pushkin, Tolstoy, Dostoevsky, Gorky, not to speak of such writers as Byelinsky or Chernyshevsky, each was something of a political institution in his day. On the other hand, many of the leaders of the revolutionary movements were men of letters. When Trotsky was once asked why Soviet Russia had no literary critic of the calibre of a Byelinsky, he answered that the new Byelinskys sat on the Politbureau and had not enough time for literary pursuits. Stalin expelled the Byelinskys from the Politbureau and from literature; and he exterminated them. But Trotsky's observation was essentially correct: the Russian man of letters is potentially a political spokesman; and any ferment of ideas in literature affects contagiously the political atmosphere in the country.

Let us now survey briefly the issues which have stood in the centre of the literary debates and consider their significance.

To outsiders it may appear odd that the debates reached the highest pitch of political passion when one literary critic, V. Pomerantsev, published an essay saying that the test by which a work of literature must be judged is whether it expresses a *sincere* emotion or not. To treat sincerity as the criterion of artistic value is hardly a new or a very sophisticated idea. An essay like Pomerantsev's would scarcely have given rise to a *cause célèbre* outside Russia. But in Russia this exaltation of sincerity has had the effect of a bombshell. After the terrified hush-hush of so many years, Russia's political acoustics have become very sensitive, so that now even fairly innocent words may sound like a call to revolt. Implicitly, Pomerantsev has denounced the literary output of the Stalin era as a product of hypocrisy, and this alone would have been enough to set against him multitudes of axe-grinders. He has also tried to substitute the test of sincerity for the accepted tests of ideological reliability and political loyalty. Unwittingly perhaps, he suggested that for a Soviet writer to be loyal meant to be hypocritical, or, at any rate, that disloyalty may be redeemed if there is a sincere emotion behind it. This is how the party leaders have understood him, and how the reading public, too, was bound to understand him.

Pomerantsev has been silenced and denounced,

although the denunciation has been couched in terms far less severe than those that were customary in Stalin's days. The party spokesmen have argued that the need for sincerity is taken for granted but that it is intolerable that the test of sincerity should be set against the tests of truth and devotion to the communist cause. And hosts of propagandists and writers are engaged in a drive against 'Pomerantsevism'. Nobody who does not wish to forfeit respectability will now come out to defend that old frail lady, sincerity.

But before the drive against Pomerantsev had begun sincerity was by no means defenceless. To her rescue rushed enthusiastically the undergraduates of the Universities of Moscow and the *Komsomoltsy*. They swamped the desk of the editor of the *Komsomolskaya Pravda* with letters ardently supporting Pomerantsev's 'thesis'; and some of the the letters got printed. For weeks the lecture halls of the universities and the clubs and locals of the *Komsomol* resounded with passionate pleas for Pomerantsev.

This seems to have been the critical point of the story. The *Komsomoltsy* protested not only against the stereotypes of the Soviet novel, its lifeless heroes, its unconvincing plots, and its 'ideologically correct' happy endings. By allusion, or perhaps even directly, they also criticized the accepted conventions of political life, conventions equally artificial and equally 'lacking in sincerity'. They blamed the literary mirror and also the political reality it mirrored. Older people had taken the new promise of a freer era with a dose of incredulity and caution: they had burnt their fingers before. The teen-agers, on the contrary, reacted with an ardour and flamboyance by which the party leaders were taken aback. Official spokesmen have, in fact, declared that the last occasion when a similar outburst of youthful rebelliousness was witnessed in Moscow was thirty years ago when — oh, horror! — Moscow's undergraduates acclaimed Trotsky's tirades against the 'degenerate' party bureaucracy. Unfortunate boys and girls! After the intellectual slump of the Stalin era a Pomerantsev was enough to kindle their enthusiasm! Yet despite its crudity, this adolescent riot will probably be remembered as a blow struck by Russia's youth at the Byzantine hypocrisy bequeathed by Stalinism.

The next controversial issue, which may also seem odd to outsiders, ostensibly concerns only the theatre. Even in Stalin's day the public, the critics, the actors, and the producers had already grumbled about 'the lack of real conflict' in the contemporary Soviet drama; and this lack has since come to be recognized as the main fault of the contemporary Soviet play. In the Russian theatre the performance of a classical play is usually a sublime artistic festival. But the same theatre is transformed into a pit of boredom the moment a contemporary play is put on the stage. Now the audience has as if risen to boo and to hiss; and the booing and hissing are echoed by the literary and theatrical periodicals.

Here again a political issue looms in the background. The theatre pays the penalty of monolithic politics. No real contemporary conflict can be acted on the stage when no such conflict is permitted or admitted in life. Rather unfairly, the playwright is asked to solve a problem the solution of which lies ultimately in the hands of political leaders. The official view is still that there cannot and does not exist any antagonism between the various classes and groups of this allegedly classless society, between worker and peasant, manager and bureaucrat, party man and non-party man, or between ruler and ruled, and young and old, not to speak of any conflict between the sexes. The monolithic régime has been designed precisely to veil and to suppress existing social antagonisms, and to keep them below the surface of the national mind. Society is not allowed to become aware of the nature of its inner conflicts, to let those conflicts run their course, or to seek consciously a solution to them. Soviet drama has thus been denied its nourishment and life-blood, and, not surprisingly, it has been withering from pernicious anaemia.

From this point the literary debate has shifted to the problem of the 'positive hero' and the villain in current literature. Here again the literary debate touches the very springs of Soviet morale. Whether a literature succeeds in producing 'a positive hero' and whether that hero evokes response depends, apart from the writer's power of artistic presentation, on whether the ideals and virtues embodied in the hero carry conviction with a given environment, and whether they correspond with its mood. Under dictation the literature of the Stalin era tried to portray the ruling group as the paragon of virtue; and so its characters could not be animated by genuine emotion or invested with psychological truth: they had always to move and speak and behave in accordance with the latest party resolution or government decree. As Pomerantsev put it, readers of the Soviet novel 'have been deafened by the triumphant roar of tractors'; and in this roar were drowned the cries, the groans, the sighs, and the rejoicings of the human being. The 'positive hero' has been an automaton driven by a false official optimism; and the present demand for a hero with genuine emotional experience is part of a revulsion against the crudity of that 'optimism'.

An official spokesman and laureate, Konstantin Simonov, writes in *Pravda*: 'We have often shown our positive heroes in a vacuum. We have laid out with carpets the road on which they were to walk, and with our own hands we have removed from it all obstacles and have evened out all the humps and bumps. Sometimes we have taken the villains by their hands and led them off the broad road on which our positive hero was about to march. Thus we have done away with the genuine difficulties which are encountered in any struggle against evil and backwardness.' The novelistic 'heroes' were, of course, modelled on the bureaucratic leaders of the Stalin era who also 'moved in a vacuum', making sure that no hurdles and no humps and bumps of opposition were in the way.

Reacting against this, Soviet writers have recently produced a crop of novels and dramas with villains as their chief characters. As was to be expected, the reaction took an extreme and crude form, and it has been all the more revealing for that. As a rule, the villain is only yesterday's hero turned inside out. More often than not he is a member of the dominant and privileged social group shown as corrupt, opportunist, and cynical. Even official critics have sometimes admitted that the villain appears more alive and psychologically convincing than the 'positive hero'. Yet there is still no sign of any 'real conflict', for the villain finds no worthy antagonist in any positive character. In a few cases the only positive type is a survivor of the Old Guard of the revolution, once the butt of the Stalinist satire, who is now portrayed wistfully as a character of moving if somewhat anachronistic nobility and is poignantly contrasted with the young bureaucrat and careerist. This streak of nostalgia after the early days of the revolution comes sometimes very clearly to the surface. In one of the most hotly debated novels, *Seasons of the Year* by V. Panova, the characters are full-blooded and alive in the early days of the revolution, but become shadowy and fade as soon as they move into the Stalin era. A *Pravda* critic remarks that the mere transfer from the one era to the other seems to cast a blight on Panova's every character; and that only the criminal types are an exception: they flourish throughout. Consequently, he says, the moral outlook of Soviet society 'resembles the landscape of an Arabian desert'.

This revelation of the real temper of an important section of writers and artists has caused alarm in the ruling group. The well-known poets and novelists, Tvardovsky and Panferov, who edited *Novyi Mir* and *Oktyabr*, leading monthlies which have been the mouthpieces of the literary opposition, have been dismissed from their posts. But the suppression has been half-hearted by Stalinist standards; and so far it has affected only the extreme manifestations of opposition. The debate still goes on between party spokesmen and those writers who have voiced discontent in a more moderate manner.

A most instructive exchange has taken place between Ilya Ehrenburg and Konstantin Simonov in connection with Ehrenburg's *The Thaw*. Ehrenburg's chief character is a painter, Vladimir Pukhov, who has wasted his artistic personality through the constant adaptation of his gift and craft to prevalent tastes and prejudices. Pukhov is painfully aware of his decline, and in Russian fashion he indulges in restless morbid self-exposure, which does not prevent him, however, from going on with his opportunistic pot-boiling. It is difficult to withstand the impression that Pukhov is a pathetic projection of Ehrenburg himself who was once a novelist of considerable talent. 'In present circumstances', Pukhov-Ehrenburg holds, 'it is nonsensical to speak of the love of art, and it is impossible to engage in genuine art.' Ehrenburg produces a whole gallery of frustrated and embittered artists, and the situations he depicts are reminiscent of older novels describing the tragedy of the artist in Victorian society. 'All here are tacking about and dodging and telling lies, some cleverly, others stupidly.' 'They do not pay for ideas—if you have any ideas you can only break your neck.' 'The injured are not liked by us—we trust only the successful': these are some of the epigrams of the disillusioned Pukhov-Ehrenburg.

The official critics have not denied the truth of Ehrenburg's picture as far as it goes. Simonov writes: 'It is also true that in our visual arts we have had and still have too much official pomposity. . . . We have seen too many idealized portraits, too many medals, uniforms, gala dresses, and too little thought and human warmth on faces . . . too little of the life of ordinary people, of their workaday experience, love, and friendship.' What Simonov reproaches Ehrenburg with is that he treats Pukhov with too much sympathy, as a victim of Soviet society, not one of its drones; and that by failing to bring to life a single positive character, Ehrenburg has overdrawn the picture in a hue of unrelieved gloom. Finally, Simonov hints that the emotional exaggerations of the literary opposition strengthen only the hands of the defenders of the Stalinist *status quo*.

The cry for 'real conflict' and for genuine heroes and villains will not die down soon. It has its origin in an urge felt by the intelligentsia, and far beyond the intelligentsia's ranks, for a revision and redefinition of the accepted ideals and values. The cry testifies to the restless search of post-Stalin society for its own moral, political, and cultural identity. This is a difficult and in part a tragic search which is likely to go on for years. What it does demonstrate is that the society which is emerging from three decades of Stalinism has little resemblance to that of Orwell's *1984*. Its creative impulses and longings have not been destroyed under the crushing pressure of thought control. Flattened and cramped, they are nevertheless throbbing and stirring.